# MURPHY'S
# LAW

Also by Arthur Bloch

*Murphy's Law and Other Reasons Why Things Go Wrong*
*Murphy's Law, Book 2, More Reasons Why Things Go Wrong*
*Murphy's Law, Book 3, Wrong Reasons Why Things Go More*
*Complete Murphy's Law*
*Murphy's Law 2000*
*Murphy's Law Doctors*
*Murphy's Law Lawyers*
*Healing Yourself with Wishful Thinking*

# MURPHY'S LAW

*The 25th Anniversary Edition*

ARTHUR BLOCH

A Perigee Book

Most Perigee Books are available at special quantity discounts for bulk purchases for sales promotions, premiums, fund-raising or educational use. Special books, or book excerpts, can also be created to fit specific needs.

For details, write: Special Markets, The Berkley Publishing Group, 375 Hudson Street, New York, New York 10014.

**P**

A Perigee Book
Published by The Berkley Publishing Group
A division of Penguin Group (USA) Inc.
375 Hudson Street
New York, New York 10014

Perigee ISBN: 0399-52930-6

First edition: November 2003

Library of Congress Cataloging-in-Publication Data

Bloch, Arthur, 1948–
Murphy's law / Arthur Bloch,—26th anniversary ed.
p. cm.
ISBN 0-399-52930-6
1. Murphy's law—Humor. I. Title.

PN6231.M82B564 2003
818'.5402—dc22          2003060896.

Printed in the United States of America
10 9 8 7 6 5 4 3 2 1

# CoNTenTS

# iNTRoDUCTiON

**mur•phol•o•gy,** mûr-fŏl'ŏġy, *n.* **1.** The branch of knowledge relating to things going wrong. **2.** The science of error. **3.** The gathering of sayings in this area and the repetition of such. (1)>Ir. Am. *murph(y)-+>*L. —*ologia>*G. —*ologia, legō* speak; (2)>Ir. Am. *murph(y)-+>*L. —*ologia>*G. —*ologia, legō,* gather]

A lot can go wrong in a quarter of a century. As technology lunges forward, dragging us along kicking and screaming, it is no surprise that Murphy's Law has become a global phenomenon such as only its publishers—and your humble author—could have dreamed.

Since the 1977 printing of the first volume, the *Murphy's Law* books have been published in more than thirty countries in some twenty-seven languages. People all over the world now speak of *La Ley de Murphy, Murphyn Laki, La*

*Leggi di Murphy, Murphy Törvénykönyve, A Lei de Murphy,*
역자 李仁植 소개, *Murphyho Zákony, Murphy's Gesetz,*
マーフィーの法則, *Prawa Murphy'ego, Murphy's Lag,* etc.

The initial volume included, for the first time in print, the
story of the origin of Murphy's Law. This scoop came about
because of a fortunate (therefore, aberrant) set of circumstances. Prior to the book's publication, a preview was included in the best-selling *The Book of Lists.* This led to a
timely letter from Mr. George Nichols of California. We
reprint it here:

*Dear Arthur Bloch,*
*Understand you are going to publish a book,* Murphy's
Law—and Other Reasons Why Things Go Wrong. *Are you
interested in including the true story of the naming of Murphy's Law?*

*The event occurred in 1949 at Edwards Air Force Base,
Muroc, California, during Air Force Project MX981. This
was Colonel J. P. Stapp's experimental crash research testing
on the track at North Base. The work was being accomplished by Northrop Aircraft, under contract from Aero
Medical Lab at Wright Field. I was Northrop's project manager.*

*The Law's namesake was Captain Ed Murphy, a devel-
opment engineer from Wright Field Aircraft Lab. Frustra-
tion with a strap transducer which was malfunctioning due
to an error in wiring the strain gage bridges caused him to
remark—"If there is any way to do it wrong, he will"—re-*

*ferring to the technician who had wired the bridges at the Lab. I assigned Murphy's Law to the statement and the associated variations.*

*. . . A couple of weeks after the "naming," Colonel Stapp indicated, at a press conference, that our fine safety record during several years of simulated crash-force testing was the result of a firm belief in Murphy's Law, and our consistent effort to deny the inevitable. The widespread reference to the Law in manufacturers' ads within only a few months was fantastic—and Murphy's Law was off and running wild.*

*Sincerely,*

*George E. Nichols*

*Reliability & Quality Assurance Mgr.*

*Viking Project*

*Jet Propulsion Lab—NASA*

Perhaps there's more detail there than we signed up for, but the salient point is this: Murphy's Law was a misquote. Should this really be much of a surprise?

A recent Google search for Murphy's Law yielded more than 110,000 Web pages. It would be cute to say that back in 1977 there were none, but this isn't exactly true. For one of the first compilations of Laws I ever came across was a long, pin-fed, fan-fold list from the Arpinet, a precursor to the Internet that was used mostly by universities, research facilities, and government agencies. The Laws have always been popular among "nerds," even when this term had yet to be coined.

But when I submitted the first manuscript to a publisher there was an interesting stipulation. All book manuscripts must be typed. Printing by computer was not allowed. (Not that I had one—personal computers had not yet been invented.) There was a feeling then, which has never been disproven, that people writing on computers tend to lack literary discipline. These days, of course, book contracts specify that manuscripts be submitted in MSWord. My last five books have all been sent to the publisher via e-mail. This one, for some reason, requires that I do it the old-fashioned way—on a three-and-a-half-inch floppy disk.

The present volume contains the best from the many previous *Murphy's Law* books, in addition to a selection of new material. The future, in Murphological terms, is a vast and largely unimagined new world of things that can go wrong. It's good to know there will always be something to write about.

Arthur Bloch
Oakland, California

# GENeRAL mURPHology

**Murphy's Law**

If anything can go wrong, it will.

*Corollaries*

1. Nothing is as easy as it looks.
2. Everything takes longer than you think it will.
3. If there is a possibility of several things going wrong, the one that will cause the most damage will be the one to go wrong.
4. If you perceive that there are four possible ways in which a procedure can go wrong, and circumvent these, then a fifth way will promptly develop.
5. Left to themselves, things tend to go from bad to worse.
6. Whenever you set out to do something, something else must be done first.
7. Every solution breeds new problems.

8. It is impossible to make anything foolproof because fools are so ingenious.
9. Mother nature is a bitch.

## Benedict's Principle
*(formerly Murphy's Ninth Corollary)*
Nature always sides with the hidden flaw.

## Schnatterly's Summing-up of the Corollaries
If anything can't go wrong, it will.

## Bloch's Corollary
If everything can go wrong, it will.

## Leahy's Law
If a thing is done wrong often enough, it becomes right.

## Addendum to Murphy's Law
You never run out of things that can go wrong.

## Dr. Who's Rule
First things first, but not necessarily in that order.

## Murphy's Comment
When things go wrong, don't go with them.

## O'Toole's Commentary on Murphy's Law
Murphy was an optimist.

## Chisholm's First Law
When things are going well, something will go wrong.
*Corollaries*
1. When things just can't get any worse, they will.
2. Anytime things appear to be going better, you have overlooked something.

## Scott's First Law
No matter what goes wrong, it will probably look right.

## Silverman's Paradox
If Murphy's Law can go wrong, it will.

## Sodd's First Law
When a person attempts a task, he will be thwarted in that task by the unconscious intervention of some other presence (animate or inanimate). Nevertheless, some tasks are completed, since the intervening presence is itself attempting a task and is, of course, subject to interference.

## Sodd's Second Law
Sooner or later, the worst possible set of circumstances is bound to occur.
*Corollary*
Any system must be designed to withstand the worst possible set of circumstances.

## Simon's Law
Everything put together falls apart sooner or later.

## Rudin's Law
In crises that force people to choose among alternative courses of action, most people will choose the worst one possible.

## Murphy's Law of Thermodynamics
Things get worse under pressure.

## Nichols's Fourth Law
Avoid any action with an unacceptable outcome.

## Commoner's Law of Ecology
Nothing ever goes away.

## Pudder's Law
Anything that begins well ends badly.
Anything that begins badly ends worse.

## Stockmayer's Theorem
If it looks easy, it's tough.
If it looks tough, it's damn well impossible.

## Zymurgy's Law of Evolving Systems Dynamics
Once you open a can of worms, the only way to recan them is to use a larger can.

## Kaiser's Comment on Zymurgy
Never open a can of worms unless you plan to go fishing.

## Sturgeon's Law
Ninety percent of everything is crud.

## The Unspeakable Law
As soon as you mention something
   —if it's good, it goes away.
   —if it's bad, it happens.

## Nonreciprocal Laws of Expectations
Negative expectations yield negative results.
Positive expectations yield negative results.

## Nagler's Comment on the Origin of Murphy's Law
Murphy's Law was not propounded by Murphy, but by another man of the same name.

## Kohn's Corollary to Murphy's Law
Two wrongs are only the beginning.

## McDonald's Corollary to Murphy's Law
In any given set of circumstances, the proper course of action is determined by subsequent events.

## Murphy's Law of Government
If anything can go wrong, it will do so in triplicate.

**Maahs's Law**
Things go right so they can go wrong.

**Murphy's Uncertainty Principle**
You can know something has gone wrong only when you make an odd number of mistakes.

**Tussman's Law**
Nothing is as inevitable as a mistake whose time has come.

**Law of Probable Dispersal**
Whatever hits the fan will not be evenly distributed.

**Gualtieri's Law of Inertia**
Where there's a will, there's a won't.

**Fahnstock's Rule for Failure**
If at first you don't succeed, destroy all evidence that you tried.

**Evans and Bjorn's Law**
No matter what goes wrong, there is always somebody who knew it would.

**Murphy's Law of Topology**
The shortest distance between two points is a downward spiral.

## Law of Conservation of Tsouris

The amount of aggravation in the universe is a constant.

*Corollary*

If things are going well in one area, they are going wrong in another.

## Lee's Law

It takes less time to do something right than it takes to explain why you did it wrong.

## Irene's Law

There is no right way to do the wrong thing.

## Campbell's Law

The less you do, the less can go wrong.

## Stewart's Murphy Corollaries

1. Murphy's Law may be delayed or suspended for an indefinite period of time, provided that such delay or suspension will result in a greater catastrophe at a later date.
2. The magnitude of the catastrophe is directly proportional to the number of people watching.
3. The magnitude of the catastrophe is exponentially proportional to the importance of the occasion.
4. If an outcome has a 50 percent chance of occurring, its actual probability of happening is inversely proportional to the desirability of the outcome.

5. If two corollaries of Murphy's Law contradict each other, the one with greater potential for damage takes precedence.

## Fresco's Discovery
If you knew what you were doing you'd probably be bored.
*Corollary*
Just because you're bored doesn't mean you know what you're doing.

## Baldridge's Law
If we knew what we were getting into we would never get into anything.

## Golden Principle
Nothing will be attempted if all possible objections must first be overcome.

## Cooke's Law
It is always hard to notice what isn't there.

## Philo's Law
To learn from your mistakes, you must first realize that you are making mistakes.

## Wolf's Law of Planning
A good place to start from is where you are.

## Hofstadter's Law
Things always take longer than you anticipate, even if you take into account Hofstadter's Law.

## Dunn's Law
Careful planning is no substitute for dumb luck.

## Gilbertson's Law
Nothing is foolproof to a sufficiently talented fool.

## Siwiak's Rule
The only way to make something foolproof is to keep it away from fools.

## Naeser's Law
You can make it foolproof, but you can't make it damnfool proof.

## Barber's Rule
Anything worth doing is worth doing to excess.

## Melnick's Law
If at first you do succeed, try not to look too astonished.

## The Law of Eponymy
Any given Law will not be named for the person who created it.
### Corollary
It's not who said it, it's who named it.

**Keyes's First Axiom**
Any quotation that can be ~~altered~~ changed will be.

**Langsam's Laws**
1. Everything depends.
2. Nothing is always.
3. Everything is sometimes.

**Ducharme's Precept**
Opportunity always knocks at the least opportune moment.

**Flugg's Law**
When you need to knock on wood is when you realize the world's composed of aluminum and vinyl.

**First Postulate of Iso-Murphism**
Things equal to nothing else are equal to each other.

**Coit-Murphy's Statement on the Power of Negative Thinking**
It is impossible for an optimist to be pleasantly surprised.

**Ferguson's Precept**
A crisis is when you can't say "let's forget the whole thing."

**The Unapplicable Law**
Washing your car to make it rain doesn't work.

## Murphy's Saving Grace
The worst is enemy of the bad.

## The Cardinal Conundrum
An optimist believes we live in the best of all possible worlds.
A pessimist fears this is true.

## Dude's Law Duality
Of two possible events, only the undesired one will occur.

## Hane's Law
There is no limit to how bad things can get.

## Perrussel's Law
There is no job so simple that it cannot be done wrong.

## Mae West's Observation
To err is human, but it feels divine.

## Borkowski's Law
You can't guard against the arbitrary.

## Lackland's Laws
1. Never be first.
2. Never be last.
3. Never volunteer for anything.

**Higdon's Law**
Good judgment comes from bad experience.
Experience comes from bad judgment.

**The Chi Factor**
Quantity = 1/quality; or, quantity is inversely
proportional to quality.

**Frothingham's Law**
Urgency varies inversely with importance.

**The Rockefeller Principle**
Never do anything you wouldn't be caught dead doing.

**Young's Law of Inanimate Mobility**
All inanimate objects can move just enough to get in your
way.

**Meskimen's Law**
There's never time to do it right, but there's always time to
do it over.

# APpLIED mURPHology

**Booker's Law**
An ounce of application is worth a ton of abstraction.

**The Extended Murphy's Law**
If a series of events goes wrong, it will do so in the worst possible sequence.

**Farnsdick's Corollary to the Fifth Corollary**
After things have gone from bad to worse, the cycle will repeat itself.

**Gattuso's Extension of Murphy's Law**
Nothing is ever so bad that it can't get worse.

**Gumperson's Law**
The probability of anything happening is in inverse ratio to its desirability.

## Iles' Law
There is always an easier way to do it.
### Corollaries
1. When looking directly at the easier way, especially for long periods, you will not see it.
2. Neither will Iles.

## Heisenberg's Uncertainty Principle
The location of all objects cannot be known simultaneously.
### Corollary
If a lost thing is found, something else will disappear.

## Oien's Observation
The quickest way to find something is to start looking for something else.

## Maryann's Law
You can always find what you're not looking for.

## Advanced Law of the Search
The first place to look for anything is the last place you would expect to find it.

## Boob's Law
You always find something in the last place you look.

## Bloch's Rebuttal to Boob's Law
You always find something in the first place you look, but you never find it the first time you look there.

## Richard's Complementary Rules of Ownership

1. If you keep anything long enough you can throw it away.
2. If you throw anything away, you will need it as soon as it is no longer accessible.

## Gillette's Law of Household Moving

What you lost during your first move you find during your second move.

## Glatum's Law of Materialistic Acquisitiveness

The perceived usefulness of an article is inversely proportional to its actual usefulness once bought and paid for.

## Harper's Law

You never find an article until you replace it.

## MacPherson's Theory of Entropy

It requires less energy to take an object out of its proper place than to put it back.

## Schopenhauer's Law of Entropy

If you put a spoonful of wine in a barrel full of sewage, you get sewage.

If you put a spoonful of sewage in a barrel full of wine, you get sewage.

## Allen's Law
Almost anything is easier to get into than to get out of.

## Law of the Perversity of Nature
You cannot successfully determine beforehand which side of the bread to butter.

## Law of Selective Gravity
An object will fall so as to do the most damage.

### Jenning's Corollary
The chance of the bread falling with the buttered side down is directly proportional to the cost of the carpet.

### Klipstein's Corollary
The most delicate component will be the one to drop.

## Fulton's Law of Gravity
The effort to catch a falling, breakable object will produce more destruction than if the object had been allowed to fall in the first place.

## Paul's Law
You can't fall off the floor.

## Murphy's Asymmetry Principle
Things go wrong all at once, but things go right gradually.

### Corollary
It takes no time at all to break something, but it takes forever to have something repaired.

## Etorre's Observation
The other line moves faster.

## O'Brien's Variation on Etorre's Observation
If you change lines, the one you just left will start to move faster than the one you are now in.
### Kenton's Corollary
Switching back screws up both lines and makes everybody angry.

## The Queue Principle
The longer you wait in line, the greater the likelihood that you are standing in the wrong line.

## The Linear Accelerator Principle
The shorter the line, the slower it moves.

## Langer's Law
If the line moves quickly, you're in the wrong line.

## Flugg's Rule
The slowest checker is always at the quick-checkout lane.

## Vile's Law of Advanced Linesmanship
1. If you're running for a short line, it suddenly becomes a long line.
2. When you're waiting in a long line, the people behind you are shunted to a new, short line.

3. If you step out of a short line for a second, it becomes a long line.
4. If you're in a short line, the people in front let in their friends and relatives and make it a long line.
5. A short line outside a building becomes a long line inside.
6. If you stand in one place long enough, you make a line.

### Heid's Law of Lines
No matter how early you arrive, someone else is in line first.

### Luposchainsky's Hurry-Up-and-Wait Principle
If you're early, it'll be canceled.
If you knock yourself out to be on time, you will have to wait.
If you're late, you will be too late.

### Zadra's Law of Biomechanics
The severity of the itch is inversely proportional to the reach.

### R. C. Gallagher's Law
Change is inevitable—except from a vending machine.

### Yellin's Law
The probability of winning the lottery is slightly greater if you buy a ticket.

## Postal Principle
People usually get what's coming to them . . . unless it's been mailed.

## Laws of Truth in Reporting
1. The closer you are to the facts of a situation, the more obvious are the errors in the news coverage.
2. The farther you are from the facts of a situation, the more you tend to believe news coverage.

## Avery's Observation
It does not matter if you fall down as long as you pick up something from the floor while you get up.

# mURPHology OF KnOWLEDge

**Groya's Law of Epistemology**
What we learn after we know it all is what counts.

**Twain's Truth**
People believe what you say, except when you're telling the truth.

**Ginsberg's Theorem**
1. You can't win.
2. You can't break even.
3. You can't even quit the game.

**Freeman's Commentary on Ginsberg's Theorem**
Every major philosophy that attempts to make life seem meaningful is based on the negation of one part of Ginsberg's Theorem. To wit:

1. Capitalism is based on the assumption that you can win.
2. Socialism is based on the assumption that you can break even.
3. Mysticism is based on the assumption that you can quit the game.

## Clarke's First Law

When a distinguished but elderly scientist states that something is possible, he is almost certainly right. When he states that something is impossible, he is very probably wrong.

## Clarke's Second Law

The only way to discover the limits of the possible is to go beyond them into the impossible.

## Aristotle's Dictum

One should always prefer the probable impossible to the improbable possible.

## Von Braun's Advice

I have learned to use the word "impossible" with the greatest caution.

## Fagin's Rule on Past Prediction

Hindsight is an exact science.

**Dunlap's Laws of Physics**
1. Fact is solidified opinion.
2. Facts may weaken under extreme heat and pressure.
3. Truth is elastic.

**Democritus's Rule**
Nothing exists except atoms and empty space. Everything else is opinion.

**Merkin's Maxim**
When in doubt, predict that the trend will continue.

**Halgren's Solution**
When in trouble, obfuscate.

**Hawkins's Theory of Progress**
Progress does not consist in replacing a theory that is wrong with one that is right. It consists in replacing a theory that is wrong with one that is more subtly wrong.

**Hanlon's Razor**
Never attribute to malice that which is adequately explained by stupidity.

**Matz's Maxim**
A conclusion is the place where you got tired of thinking.

**Levy's First Law**
No amount of genius can overcome a preoccupation with detail.

**Law of Living**
As soon as you're doing what you wanted to be doing, you want to be doing something else.

**Olivier's Law**
Experience is something you don't get until just after you need it.

**Gabitol's Observation**
The wise are pleased when they discover truth, fools when they discover falsehood.

**The Two Rules for Ultimate Success in Life**
   1. Never tell everything you know.

**First Rule of Negative Anticipation**
You will save yourself a lot of needless worry if you don't burn your bridges until you come to them.

**Steiner's Precepts**
   1. Knowledge based on external evidence is unreliable.
   2. Logic can never decide what is possible or impossible.

## Coleridge's Law
Extremes meet.

## Feinberg's Principle
Memory serves its own master.

## Disimoni's Rule of Cognition
Believing is seeing.

## The Siddhartha Principle
You cannot cross a river in two strides.

## Kierkegaard's Observation
Life can only be understood backwards, but it must be lived forward.

## Haldane's Law
The universe is not only queerer than we imagine, it's queerer than we can imagine.

## Law of Observation
Nothing looks as good close up as it does from far away. Or—nothing looks as good from far away as it does close up.

## Cannon's Canon
Experience is what causes you to make new mistakes instead of old ones.

## Jones's Law
Experience enables you to recognize a mistake when you make it again.

## Bacon's Maxim
Truth comes out of error more easily than out of confusion.

## Bohr's Axiom
The opposite of a profound truth may well be another profound truth.

## Manly's Maxim
Logic is a systematic method of coming to the wrong conclusion with confidence.

## Phillips's Rule
The best defense against logic is ignorance.

## Sandy's Comment
It makes sense, when you don't think about it.

## Wilde on Advice
The only thing to do with good advice is pass it on. It is never any use to oneself.

## Von Neumann's Axiom
There's no sense in being precise when you don't know what you're talking about.

## Tatman's Rule
Always assume that your assumption is invalid.

## Young's Rule of Argument
They can't agree with you if you don't agree with them.

## De Beaumarchais's Motto
It is not necessary to understand things in order to argue about them.

## Weber's Maxim
A single fact can spoil a good argument.

## Gell-Mann's Dictum
Whatever isn't forbidden is required.
### Corollary
If there's no reason why something shouldn't exist, then it must exist.

## Kepler's Law of Ecology
Nature uses as little as possible of anything.

## The Rational Fallacy
Everything happens for a reason.

# PRobLEMA TicS

**Smith's Law**
No real problem has a solution.

**Hoare's Law of Large Problems**
Inside every large problem is a small problem struggling to get out.

**The Schainker Converse to**
**Hoare's Law of Large Problems**
Inside every small problem is a larger problem struggling to get out.

**Apple's Law of Recovery**
You can't recover from a problem you don't have.

**Peer's Law**
The solution to a problem changes the nature of the problem.

**Baruch's Observation**
If all you have is a hammer, everything looks like a nail.

**Fox on Problematics**
When a problem goes away, the people working to solve it do not.

**Waldrop's Principle**
The person not here is the one working on the problem.

**Biondi's Law**
If your project doesn't work, look for the part you didn't think was important.

**Sten's Axiom**
No problem is so formidable that you can't just walk away from it.

**Disraeli's Dictum**
Error is often more earnest than truth.

**The Roman Rule**
The one who says it cannot be done should never interrupt the one who is doing it.

**Blair's Observation**
The best-laid plans of mice and men are usually about equal.

**Seay's Law**
Nothing ever comes out as planned.

**Ruckert's Law**
There is nothing so small that it can't be blown out of proportion.

**Van Herpen's Law**
The solving of a problem lies in finding the solvers.

**Baxter's Law**
An error in the premise will appear in the conclusion.

**McGee's First Law**
It's amazing how long it takes to complete something you are not working on.

**Holten's Homily**
The only time to be positive is when you are positive you are wrong.

**Sevareid's Law**
The chief cause of problems is solutions.

## Ducharm's Axiom
If one views one's problem closely enough, one will recognize oneself as part of the problem.

## Kelley's Law
Nothing is ever as simple as it first seems.

## McGuffin's Law
It's easy to see the bright side of other people's problems.

## Beryl's Second Law
It's always easy to see both sides of an issue we are not particularly concerned about.

## Gardener's Philosophy
Brilliant opportunities are cleverly disguised as insolvable problems.
### Corollary
The reverse is also true.

## Issawi-Wilcox Principle
Problems increase in geometric ratio, solutions in arithmetic ratio.

## Herman's Law
A good scapegoat is almost as good as a solution.

## The Kibbitzer's Rule
It is much easier to suggest solutions when you know nothing about the problem.

## Big Al's Law
A good solution can be successfully applied to almost any problem.
### Primary Political Corollary
A good slogan beats a good solution.

## Burke's Rule
Never create a problem for which you do not have the answer.
### Corollary
Create problems for which only you have the answer.

## Mencken's Maxim
There's always an easy solution to every human problem—neat, plausible, and wrong.

## Grossman on Mencken
Complex problems have simple, easy-to-understand wrong answers.

## Barry's Rule
If you stop to think, remember to start again.

## The First Rule of Excavation
If you are in hole, stop digging.

# EXPertSMA NShiP

**Hiram's Law**
If you consult enough experts you can confirm any opinion.

**Gioia's Theory**
The person with the least expertise has the most opinions.

**Allison's Precept**
The best simpleminded test of expertise in a particular area is the ability to win money in a series of bets on future occurrences in that area.

**Weinberg's Corollary**
An expert is a person who avoids the small errors while sweeping on to the grand fallacy.

## Mars's Rule
An expert is anyone from out of town.

## Weber's Definition
An expert is one who knows more and more about less and less until he knows absolutely everything about nothing.

## Bohr's Law
An expert is someone who has made all of the possible mistakes in a very narrow field of study.

## Ryan's Law
Make three correct guesses consecutively and you will establish yourself as an expert.

## MacDonald's Law
Consultants are mystical people who ask a company for a number and then give it back to them.

## Warren's Rule
To spot the expert, pick the one who predicts the job will take the longest and cost the most.

## Winger's Rule
If it sits on your desk for fifteen minutes, you've just become the expert.

**Horowitz's Rule**
Wisdom consists of knowing when to avoid perfection.

**Green's Law of Debate**
Anything is possible if you don't know what you're talking about.

**Jong's Law**
Advice is what we ask for when we already know the answer but wish we didn't.

**De Nevers's Law of Complexity**
The simplest subjects are the ones you don't know anything about.

**Christie-Davies's Theorem**
If your facts are wrong but your logic is perfect, then your conclusions are inevitably false. Therefore, by making mistakes in your logic, you have at least a random chance of coming to a correct conclusion.

**Emerson's Observation**
In every work of genius we recognize our rejected thoughts.

**Jordan's Law**
An informant who never produces misinformation is too deviant to be trusted.

### De Nevers's Lost Law
Never speculate on that which can be known for certain.

### Van Roy's First Law
If you can distinguish between good advice and bad advice, then you don't need advice.

### Howe's Law
Everyone has a scheme that will not work.

### Munder's Corollary to Howe's Law
Everyone who does not work has a scheme that does.

### Rule of the Open Mind
People who are resistant to change cannot resist change for the worse.

### Ely's Key to Success
Create a need and fill it.

### Bralek's Rule for Success
Trust only those who stand to lose as much as you when things go wrong.

### The Golden Rule of Arts and Sciences
Whoever has the gold makes the rules.

**Malek's Law**
Any simple idea will be worded in the most complicated way.

**The Rule of the Way Out**
Always leave room to add an explanation if it doesn't work out.

**Cohen's Law**
What really matters is the name that you are able to impose upon the facts—not the facts themselves.

**Barth's Distinction**
There are two types of people: those who divide people into two types, and those who don't.

**Segal's Law**
A man with one watch knows what time it is.
A man with two watches is never sure.

**Miller's Law**
You can't tell how deep a puddle is until you step in it.

**Weiler's Law**
Nothing is impossible for the man who doesn't have to do it himself.

## Lacopi's Law
After food and sex, man's greatest drive is to tell the other fellow how to do his job.

## LaCombe's Rule of Percentages
The incidence of anything worthwhile is either 15–25 percent or 80–90 percent.
### Dudenhoefer's Corollary
An answer of 50 percent will suffice for the 40–60 range.

## Schroeder's Law
Indecision is the basis for flexibility.

## Whitehead's Rule
Seek simplicity, and distrust it.

## Mullins's Observation
Indecision is the key to flexibility.

## The Munroe Doctrine
A little inaccuracy sometimes saves tons of explanation.

## Buechner's Principle
The simplest explanation is that it just doesn't make sense.

## LaGuardia's Law
Statistics are like expert witnesses—they will testify for either side.

**Pirsig's Postulate**

Data without generalization is just gossip.

**Law of Retrospection**

You can never tell which way the train went by looking at the track.

**Utvich's Law**

One accurate measurement is worth a thousand expert opinions.

# BuREAuCRA TicS

**The Bureaucracy Principle**
Only a bureaucracy can fight a bureaucracy.

**Fox on Bureaucracy**
A bureaucracy can outwait anything.
*Corollary*
Never get caught between two bureaucracies.

**Young's Law of Bureaucracy**
It is the dead wood that holds up the tree.
*Corollary*
Just because it is still standing doesn't mean it's not dead.

**Soper's Law**
Any bureaucracy reorganized to enhance efficiency is immediately indistinguishable from its predecessor.

## Owen's Theory of Organizational Deviance
Every organization has an allotted number of positions to be filled by misfits.
### Corollary
Once a misfit leaves, another will be recruited.

## Post's Managerial Observation
The inefficiency and stupidity of the staff corresponds to the inefficiency and stupidity of the management.

## Mollison's Bureaucracy Hypothesis
If an idea can survive a bureaucratic review and be implemented, it wasn't worth doing.

## Robertson's Rule of Bureacracy
The more directives you issue to solve a problem, the worse it gets.

## Parkinson's Law of Delay
Delay is the deadliest form of denial.

## Loftus's Theory on Personnel Recruitment
1. Faraway talent always seems better than home-developed talent.
2. Personnel recruiting is a triumph of hope over experience.

## Loftus's Law of Management
Some people manage by the book, even though they don't know who wrote the book or even what the book is.

## Joe's Law
The inside contact that you have developed at great expense is the first person to be let go in any reorganization.

## The Lippman Lemma
People specialize in their area of greatest weakness.

## Things That Can Be Counted on in a Crisis
MARKETING says yes.

FINANCE says no.

LEGAL has to review it.

PERSONNEL is concerned.

PLANNING is frantic.

ENGINEERING is above it all.

MANUFACTURING wants more floor space.

TOP MANAGEMENT wants someone responsible.

## Cohn's Law
In any bureaucracy, paperwork increases as you spend more and more time reporting on the less and less you are doing. Stability is achieved when you spend all of your time reporting on the nothing you are doing.

### Sweeney's Law
The length of a progress report is inversely proportional to the amount of progress.

### Morris's Law of Conferences
The most interesting paper will be scheduled simultaneously with the second most interesting paper.

### Collins's Conference Principle
The speaker with the most monotonous voice speaks after the big meal.

### Patton's Law
A good plan today is better than a perfect plan tomorrow.

### Jacobson's Law
The less work an organization produces, the more frequently it reorganizes.

### Rule of Defactualization
Information deteriorates upward through bureaucracies.

### Acheson's Rule of the Bureaucracy
A memorandum is written not to inform the reader but to protect the writer.

## Law of Corporate Takeovers

In any corporate buyout, the resultant company will provide inferior service and quality.

*Corollaries*
1. The larger the company that takes over, the less attention is paid to projects ongoing before the takeover.
2. When they say no jobs will be lost, they are lying.

## McCarthy's Maxim

The only thing that saves us from the bureaucracy is its inefficiency.

## Adler's Axiom

Language is all that separates us from the lower animals—and from the bureaucrats.

## Gammon's Law

In a bureaucratic system, increase in expenditure will be matched by fall in production.

## Nies's Law

The effort expended by a bureaucracy in defending any error is in direct proportion to the size of the error.

## Herbert's Law

A bureaucracy is an organization that has raised stupidity to the status of a religion.

# HiErARCHIOLogy

### Aigner's Axiom
No matter how well you perform your job, a superior will seek to modify the results.

### The Pitfalls of Genius
No boss will keep an employee who is right all the time.

### Perkins's Postulate
The bigger they are, the harder they hit.

### Harrison's Postulate
For every action, there is an equal and opposite criticism.

### Rogers's Rule
Authorization for a project will be granted only when none of the authorizers can be blamed if the project fails

but when all of the authorizers can claim credit if it succeeds.

## Gates's Law
The only important information in a hierarchy is who knows what.

## Bachman's Inevitability Theorem
The greater the cost of putting a plan into operation, the less chance there is of abandoning the plan—even if it subsequently becomes irrelevant.
*Corollary*
The higher the level of prestige accorded the people behind the plan, the less, less chance there is of abandoning it.

## Conway's Law
In any organization there will always be one person who knows what is going on. This person must be fired.

## Fox on Levelology
What will get you promoted on one level will get you killed on another.

## Stewart's Law of Retroaction
It is easier to get forgiveness than permission.

## First Rule of Superior Inferiority
Don't let your superiors know you're better than they are.

## Whistler's Law
You never know who's right, but you always know who's in charge.

## Spencer's Laws of Data
1. Anyone can make a decision given enough facts.
2. A good manager can make a decision without enough facts.
3. A perfect manager can operate in perfect ignorance.

## Gottlieb's Rule
The boss who attempts to impress employees with his knowledge of intricate details has lost sight of the final objective.

## Dingle's Law
When somebody drops something, everybody will kick it around instead of picking it up.

## Kushner's Law
The chances of anybody doing anything are inversely proportional to the number of other people who are in a position to do it instead.

## Pfeifer's Principle
Never make a decision you can get someone else to make.
### Corollary
No one keeps a record of decisions you could have made but didn't. Everyone keeps a record of your bad ones.

**Thal's Law**
For every vision, there is an equal and opposite revision.

**Wellington's Law of Command**
The cream rises to the top.
So does the scum.

**Heller's Law**
The first myth of management is that it exists.
*Johnson's Corollary*
Nobody really knows what is going on anywhere within the organization.

**The Peter Principle**
In a hierarchy, every employee tends to rise to his level of incompetence.
*Corollaries*
1. In time, every post tends to be occupied by an employee who is incompetent to carry out his duties.
2. Work is accomplished by those employees who have not yet reached their level of incompetence.

**Vail's Axiom**
In any human enterprise, work seeks the lowest hierarchial level.

### Imhoff's Law
The organization of any bureaucracy is very much like a septic tank—the really big chunks always rise to the top.

### Rogers's Observation Regarding the Laws
In a bureaucratic hierarchy, the higher up the organization you go, the less people appreciate Murphy's Law, the Peter Principle, etc.

### Wilson's Law
A person's rank is in inverse relation to the speed of his speech.

### The Chief Executive in Charge of Titles Law
The longer the title, the less important the job.

### Fifth Rule of Success in Business
Keep your boss's boss off your boss's back.

### Grizzard's Sled-Dog Principle
Only the lead dog gets a change of scenery.

### Prince's Principle
People who work sitting down are paid more than people who work standing up.

### Engle's Law
When you stand up to be counted, someone will take your seat.

## Anderson's Laws of Survival for Low-Level Managers
1. Never be too right too often.
2. Hints are better taken than given.

## Second Law of the Corporation
Any action for which there is no logical explanation will be deemed "company policy."

## Chapman's Law
Don't be irreplaceable. If you can't be replaced, you can't be promoted.

## Owens's Law
If you are good, you will be assigned all the work. If you are really good, you will get out of it.

## Levin's Law
Following the rules will not get the job done.
### Corollary
Getting the job done is no excuse for not following the rules.

## Third Law of Productivity
When the bosses talk about improving productivity, they are never talking about themselves.

## The Salary Axiom
The pay raise is just large enough to increase your taxes and just small enough to have no effect on your take-home pay.

## Law of Communications
The inevitable result of improved and enlarged communications among different levels in a hierarchy is a vastly increased area of misunderstanding.

## Dow's Law
In a hierarchical organization, the higher the level, the greater the confusion.

## Buñuel's Law
Overdoing things is harmful in all cases, even when it comes to efficiency.

## Spark's Ten Rules for the Project Manager
1. Strive to look tremendously important.
2. Attempt to be seen with important people.
3. Speak with authority; however, only expound on the obvious and proven facts.
4. Don't engage in arguments, but if cornered, ask an irrelevant question and lean back with a satisfied grin while your opponent tries to figure out what's going on—then quickly change the subject.
5. Listen intently while others are arguing the problem. Pounce on a trite statement and bury them with it.
6 If a subordinate asks you a pertinent question, look at him as if he has lost his senses. When he looks down, paraphrase the question back at him.

7. Obtain a brilliant assignment, but keep out of sight and out of the limelight.
8. Walk at a fast pace when out of the office—this keeps questions from subordinates and superiors at a minimum.
9. Always keep the office door closed. This puts visitors on the defensive and also makes it look as if you are always in an important conference.
10. Give all orders verbally. Never write anything down that might go into a "Pearl Harbor File."

## Truths of Management
1. Think before you act; it's not your money.
2. No executives devote effort to proving themselves wrong.
3. If sophisticated calculations are needed to justify an action, don't do it.

## Worker's Dilemma
1. No matter how much you do, you'll never do enough.
2. What you don't do is always more important than what you do do.

## Match's Maxim
A fool in a high station is like a man on the top of a high mountain: everything appears small to him and he appears small to everybody.

## Iron Law of Distribution
Them that has, gets.

## Jones's Law
The man who can smile when things go wrong has thought of someone he can blame it on.

## Law of Socioeconomics
In a hierarchical system, the rate of pay for a given task increases in inverse ratio to the unpleasantness and difficulty of the task.

## Putt's Law
Technology is dominated by two types of people:
Those who understand what they do not manage.
Those who manage what they do not understand.

## Young's Rule of Delegation
When moving a pregnant cat, pick up the cat and let her take care of the kittens.

## Planer's Rule
An exception granted becomes a right expected the next time it is requested.

# cOMMiTTolOgY

**McKernan's Maxim**
Those who are unable to learn from past meetings are condemned to repeat them.

**Courtois's Rule**
If people listened to themselves more often, they would talk less.

**Old and Kahn's Law**
The efficiency of a committee meeting is inversely proportional to the number of participants and the time spent on deliberations.

**Shanahan's Law**
The length of a meeting rises with the square of the number of people present.

## Law of Triviality
The time spent on any item of the agenda will be in inverse proportion to the sum involved.

## Mitchell's Laws of Committology
1. Any simple problem can be made insoluble if enough conferences are held to discuss it.
2. Once the way to screw up a project is presented for consideration, it will invariably be accepted as the soundest solution.
3. After the solution screws up the project, all those who initially endorsed it will say, "I wish I had voiced my reservations at the time."

## Issawi's Law of Committo-Dynamics
The less you enjoy serving on committees, the more likely you are to be pressed to do so.

## Matilda's Law of Subcommittee Formation
If you leave the room, you're elected.

## Kim's Rule of Committees
After an hour has been spent amending a sentence, someone will move to delete the paragraph.

## The Eleventh Commandment
Thou shalt not committee.

## Kennedy's Comment on Committees
A committee is twelve people doing the work of one.

## Kirby's Comment on Committees
A committee is the only life-form with twelve stomachs and no brain.

## Burgess's Law of Committo-Dynamics
Those most opposed to serving on committees are made chairpersons.

## Hendrickson's Law
If a problem causes many meetings, the meetings eventually become more important than the problem.

## Lord Falkland's Rule
When it is not necessary to make a decision, it is necessary not to make a decision.

## Hutchins's Law
You can't outtalk someone who knows what he's talking about.

## Hartz's Law of Rhetoric
Any argument carried far enough will end up in semantics.

## Gourd's Axiom
A meeting is an event at which the minutes are kept and the hours are lost.

## First Law of Business Meetings
The lead in a pencil will break in direct proportion to the importance of the notes being taken.

## Second Law of Business Meetings
If there are two possible ways to spell a person's name, you will pick the wrong spelling.

## Truman's Law
If you cannot convince them, confuse them.

## First Law of Debate
Never argue with a fool—people might not know the difference.

## Swipple's Rule of Order
He who shouts loudest has the floor.

## De Nevers's Law of Debate
Two monologues do not make a dialogue.

## Rayburn's Rule
If you want to get along, go along.

## Boren's Laws
1. When in doubt, mumble.
2. When in trouble, delegate.
3. When in charge, ponder.

## Van Roy's Law
A meeting is no substitute for progress.

## Phillip's Law of Committee Procedure
The only changes that are easily adopted are changes for the worse.

## Cocks's Comment
A committee is a cul-de-sac down which ideas are lured and then quietly strangled.

## Coblitz's Law
A committee can make a decision that is dumber than any of its members.

## Lucas's Law
No one has ever erected a monument to a committee.

## Trahey's Law
Never dump a good idea on a conference table. It will belong to the conference.

## Peterson's Principle
Never delay the ending of a meeting or the beginning of a dinner hour.

## Chapman's Committee Rules

1. Never arrive on time, or you will be stamped a beginner.
2. Don't say anything until the meeting is half over; this stamps you as being wise.
3. Be as vague as possible; this prevents irritating others.
4. When in doubt, suggest that a subcommittee be appointed.
5. Be the first to move for adjournment; this will make you popular—it's what everyone is waiting for.

## Horwood's Eighth Law

In complex systems, there is no relationship between information gathered and decisions made.

## Wolinski's Law

Teamwork is wasting half of one's time explaining to others why they are wrong.

## Parker's Rule of Parliamentary Procedure

A motion to adjourn is always in order.

# ACCoUNTSManSHIp

**Parks's Law of Insurance Rates and Taxes**
Whatever goes up, stays up.

**First Law of Money Dynamics**
A surprise monetary windfall will be accompanied by an unexpected expense of the same amount.

**Spencer's Laws of Accountancy**
1. Trial balances don't.
2. Working capital doesn't.
3. Liquidity tends to run out.
4. Return on investments won't.

**Frothingham's Fallacy**
Time is money.

## Westheimer's Rule

To estimate the time it takes to do a task, estimate the time you think it should take, multiply by two, and change the unit of measure to the next highest unit. Thus we allocate two days for a one-hour task.

## Edwards's Time/Effort Law

Effort × Time = Constant

1. Given a large initial time to do something, the initial effort will be small.
2. As time goes to zero, effort goes to infinity.

*Corollary*

If it weren't for the last minute, nothing would get done.

## Gresham's Law

Trivial matters are handled promptly; important matters are never solved.

## Gray's Law of Programming

"N+1" trivial tasks are expected to be accomplished in the same time as "n" tasks.

## The 90/90 Rule of Project Schedules

The first 90 percent of the task takes 10 percent of the time, and the last 10 percent takes the other 90.

## Weinberg's Law

Progress is made on alternate Fridays.

## The Ordering Principle
Those supplies necessary for yesterday's project must be ordered no later than tomorrow noon.

## Cheops's Law
Nothing ever gets built on schedule or within budget.

## Extended Epstein-Heisenberg Principle
In an R&D orbit, only two of the existing three parameters can be defined simultaneously. The parameters are task, time, and resources ($).

1. If one knows what the task is, and there is a time limit allowed for the completion of the task, then one cannot guess how much it will cost.
2. If the time and resources are clearly defined, then it is impossible to know what part of the R&D task will be performed.
3. If you are given a clearly defined R&D goal and a definite amount of money that has been calculated to be necessary for the completion of the task, you cannot predict if and when the goal will be reached.

   If one is lucky enough and can accurately define all three parameters, then what one deals with is not in the realm of R&D.

## Pareto's Law (The 20/80 Law)
Twenty percent of the customers account for 80 percent of the turnover.

Twenty percent of the components account for 80 percent of the cost, etc.

## O'Brien's Principle (The $357.73 Theory)
Auditors always reject any expense account with a bottom line divisible by five or ten.

## John's Collateral Corollary
In order to get a loan you must first prove you don't need it.

## Brien's Law
At some time in the life cycle of virtually every organization, its ability to succeed in spite of itself runs out.

## Law of Institutions
The opulence of the front-office decor varies inversely with the fundamental solvency of the firm.

## Linton's Law
Growth is directly proportional to promises made; profit is inversely proportional to promises kept.

## Gerard's Law
When there are sufficient funds in the checking account, checks take two weeks to clear. When there are insufficient funds, checks clear overnight.

## Juhani's Law
The compromise will always be more expensive than either of the suggestions it is compromising.

## Ruane's Law of Monetary Windfalls
Pennies from heaven are soon followed by a tax collector from hell.

## The Luncheon Law
The person who suggests splitting the bill evenly is always the person who ordered the most expensive meal.

## Laws of Bank Mergers
1. What's good for your bank is not good for you.
2. Your local branch will be the first one closed.

## Law of Checks and Balances
In matters of dispute, the bank's balance is always smaller than yours.

## The Callaways's Lament
Nothing in the known universe travels faster than a bad check.

## Firth's Theorem
Five is a sufficiently close approximation to infinity.

**Wincorn's Law**

There are three kinds of people. Those who can count and those who can't.

**The Fauvre Principle**

Money earned in your own business will be lost in someone else's business.

# DeSIGnSMAnSHIP

**Principle of Design Inertia**
Any change looks terrible at first.

**Eng's Principle**
The easier it is to do, the harder it is to change.

**Reisner's Rule of Conceptual Inertia**
If you think big enough, you'll never have to do it.

**Poulsen's Prophecy**
If anything is used to its full potential, it will break.

**Mayne's Law**
Nobody notices the big errors.

## Robertson's Law
Quality assurance doesn't.

## Wright's Law of Quality
Quality is inversely proportional to the time left for completion of the project.

## Law of Corporate Planning
Anything that can be changed will be changed until there is no time left to change anything.

## Seventh Law of Product Design
No problem is so large that it can't be fit in somewhere.

## Beach's Law
No two identical parts are alike.

## The Basic Law of Construction
Cut it large and kick it into place.

## Meissner's Law
Any producing entity is the last to use its own product.

## Schrank's First Law
If it doesn't work, expand it.
### Corollary
The greater the magnitude, the less notice will be taken that it does not work.

**Bitton's Postulate on State-of-the-Art Electronics**
If you understand it, it's obsolete.

**Jose's Axiom**
Nothing is as temporary as that which is called permanent.
*Corollary*
Nothing is as permanent as that which is called temporary.

**Osborn's Law**
Variables won't; constants aren't.

**First Law of Revision**
Information necessitating a change of design will be conveyed to the designer after—and only after—the plans are complete. (Often called the "Now they tell us!" Law.)
*Corollary*
In simple cases, presenting one obvious right way versus one obvious wrong way, it is often wiser to choose the wrong way, so as to expedite subsequent revision.

**Second Law of Revision**
The more innocuous the modification appears to be, the further its influence will extend and the more plans will have to be redrawn.

### Third Law of Revision
If, when completion of a design is imminent, field dimensions are finally supplied as they actually are—instead of as they were meant to be—it is always simpler to start all over.
#### Corollary
It is usually impractical to worry beforehand about interferences—if you have none, someone will make one for you.

### Law of the Lost Inch
In designing any type of construction, no overall dimension can be totaled correctly after 4:40 P.M. on Friday.
#### Corollaries
1. Under the same conditions, if any minor dimensions are given to sixteenths of an inch, they cannot be totaled at all.
2. The correct total will become self-evident at 9:01 A.M. on Monday.

### Gore's Laws of Design Engineering
1. The primary function of the design engineer is to make things difficult for the fabricator and impossible for the serviceman.
2. That component of any circuit which has the shortest service life will be placed in the least accessible location.

### Last Law of Product Design
If you can't fix it, feature it.

**Fifth Law of Design**
Design flaws travel in groups.

**Sloan's Law**
The changes in new models should be so attractive as to create dissatisfaction with past models.

**Randy's Rule**
A ton of anything is ugly.

# REseARCHMAnSHIP

**Gordon's Law**
If a research project is not worth doing at all, it is not worth doing well.

**Williams and Holland's Law**
If enough data is collected, anything may be proven by statistical methods.

**Edington's Theory**
The number of different hypotheses erected to explain a given biological phenomenon is inversely proportional to the available knowledge.

**Harvard's Law**
Under the most rigorously controlled conditions of pres-

sure, temperature, volume, humidity, and other variables, the organism will do as it damn well pleases.

## Fourth Law of Revision
After painstaking and careful analysis of a sample, you are always told that it is the wrong sample and doesn't apply to the problem.

## Finagle's First Law
If an experiment works, something has gone wrong.

## Finagle's Second Law
No matter what the anticipated result, there will always be someone eager to (a) misinterpret it, (b) fake it, or (c) believe it happened to his own pet theory.

## Finagle's Third Law
In any collection of data, the figure most obviously correct, beyond all need of checking, is the mistake.
### Corollaries
1. No one whom you ask for help will see it.
2. Everyone who stops by with unsought advice will see it immediately.

## Finagle's Fourth Law
Once a job is fouled up, anything done to improve it only makes it worse.

### Finagle's Rules
1. To study a subject best, understand it thoroughly before you start.
2. Always keep a record of data—it indicates you've been working.
3. Always draw your curves, then plot your reading.
4. In case of doubt, make it sound convincing.
5. Experiments should be reproducible—they should all fail in the same way.
6. Do not believe in miracles—rely on them.

### Wingo's Axiom
All Finagle Laws may be bypassed by learning the simple art of doing without thinking.

### Rule of Accuracy
When working toward the solution of a problem, it always helps if you know the answer.

### Young's Law
All great discoveries are made by mistake.
*Corollary*
The greater the funding, the longer it takes to make the mistake.

### Parkinson's Law for Medical Research
Successful research attracts the bigger grant, which makes further research impossible.

**Fett's Law of the Lab**
Never replicate a successful experiment.

**Wyszowski's Law**
No experiment is reproducible.

**Tenenbaum's Law of Replicability**
The most interesting results happen only once.

**Souder's Law**
Repetition does not establish validity.

**Futility Factor**
No experiment is ever a complete failure—it can always serve as a negative example.

**Parkinson's Law**
The progress of science varies inversely with the number of journals published.

**Freivald's Law**
Only a fool can reproduce another fool's work.

**Hanggi's Law**
The more trivial your research, the more people will read it and agree.
*Corollary*
The more vital your research, fewer people will understand it.

## Handy Guide to Modern Science

1. If it's green or it wriggles, it's biology.
2. If it stinks, it's chemistry.
3. If it doesn't work, it's physics.

## Cerf's Extensions to the
## Handy Guide to Modern Science

4. If it's incomprehensible, it's mathematics.
5. If it doesn't make sense, it's either economics or psychology.

## First Law of Particle Physics

The shorter the life of the particle, the more it costs to produce.

## Second Law of Particle Physics

The basic building blocks of matter do not occur in nature.

## Felson's Law

To steal ideas from one person is plagiarism; to steal from many is research.

## Pavlu's Rules for Economy in Research

1. Deny the last-established truth on the list.
2. Add yours.
3. Pass the list.

## Law of Laboratory Work

Hot glass looks exactly the same as cold glass.

## Ground Rule for Laboratory Workers
When you do not know what you are doing, do it neatly.

## Finagle's Rule
Teamwork is essential. It allows you to blame someone else.

## Finagle's Creed
Science is true. Don't be misled by facts.

## May's Law of Stratigraphy
The quality of correlation is inversely proportional to the density of control.

## Vesilind's Law of Experimentation
1. If reproducibility may be a problem, conduct the test only once.
2. If a straight line fit is required, obtain only two data points.

## Lerman's Law of Technology
Any technical problem can be overcome given enough time and money.

### Lerman's Corollary
You are never given enough time or money.

## Rocky's Lemma of Innovation Prevention
Unless the results are known in advance, funding agencies will reject the proposal.

## Sy's Law of Science

Sometimes it takes several years to recognize the obvious.

## Schingman's Guide to Medical Jargon

"IT HAS LONG BEEN KNOWN" . . . I didn't look up the original reference.

"A DEFINITE TREND IS EVIDENT" . . . These data are practically meaningless.

"WHILE IT HAS NOT BEEN POSSIBLE TO PROVIDE DEFINITE ANSWERS TO THE QUESTIONS" . . . An unsuccessful experiment, but I still hope to get it published.

"THREE OF THE SAMPLES WERE CHOSEN FOR DETAILED STUDY" . . . The other results didn't make any sense.

"TYPICAL RESULTS ARE SHOWN" . . . This is the prettiest graph.

"THESE RESULTS WILL BE IN A SUBSEQUENT REPORT" . . . I might get around to this sometime, if pushed/funded.

"THE MOST RELIABLE RESULTS ARE OBTAINED BY JONES" . . . He was my graduate student; his grade depended on this.

"IN MY EXPERINCE" . . . once.

"IN CASE AFTER CASE" . . . twice.

"IN A SERIES OF CASES" . . . thrice.

"IT IS BELIEVED THAT" . . . I think.

"IT IS GENERALLY BELIEVED THAT" . . . A couple of other guys think so, too.

"CORRECT WITHIN AN ORDER OF MAGNITUDE" . . . Wrong.

"ACCORDING TO STATISTICAL ANALYSIS" . . . Rumor has it.

"A STATISTICALLY ORIENTED PROJECTION OF THE SIGNIFI-
CANCE OF THESE FINDINGS" . . . A wild guess.

"A CAREFUL ANALYSIS OF OBTAINABLE DATA" . . . Three
pages of notes were obliterated when I knocked over a
glass of beer.

"IT IS CLEAR THAT MUCH ADDITIONAL WORK WILL BE RE-
QUIRED BEFORE A COMPLETE UNDERSTANDING OF THIS
PHENOMENA OCCURS" . . . I don't understand it.

"AFTER ADDITIONAL STUDY BY MY COLLEAGUES" . . . They
don't understand it either.

"THANKS ARE DUE TO JOE BLOTZ FOR ASSISTANCE WITH THE
EXPERIMENT AND TO ANDREA SHAEFFER FOR VALUABLE
DISCUSSIONS" . . . Mr. Boltz did the work and Ms. Sha-
effer explained to me what it meant.

"A HIGHLY SIGNIFICANT AREA FOR EXPLORATORY STUDY" . . .
A totally useless topic selected by my committee.

"IT IS HOPED THAT THIS STUDY WILL STIMULATE FURTHER IN-
VESTIGATION IN THIS FIELD" . . . I quit.

## Bates's Law of Research
Research is the process of going up alleys to see if they're blind.

## Von Braun's Credo
Research is what I'm doing when I don't know what I'm doing.

## Westheimer's Discovery
A couple of months in the laboratory can frequently save a
couple of hours in the library.

## Land's Lemma
When the experiment doesn't work, distrust the experiment; when the experiment works, distrust the theory.

## Bershader's Law
Experiment and theory often show remarkable agreement when performed in the same laboratory.

## Alan's Law of Research
The theory is supported as long as the funds are.

## Horwood's Sixth Law
If you have the right data you have the wrong problem.

## Proof Techniques
1. Proof by referral to nonexistent authorities
2. Reduction ad nauseam
3. Proof by assignment
4. Method of least astonishment
5. Proof by handwaving
6. Proof by intimidation
7. Method of deferral until later in the course
8. Proof by reduction to a sequence of unrelated lemmas
9. Method of convergent irrelevancies

## McFee's Maxim
Matter can neither be created nor destroyed. However, it can be lost.

# TECHno-mURPHology

**Klipstein's Laws Applied to General Engineering**

1. A patent application will be preceded by a similar application submitted one week earlier by an independent worker.

2. Firmness of delivery dates is inversely proportional to the tightness of the schedule.

3. Dimensions will always be expressed in the least usable term. Velocity, for example, will be expressed in furlongs per fortnight.

4. Any wire cut to length will be too short.

**Applied to Prototyping and Production**

1. Tolerances will accumulate unidirectionally toward maximum difficulty to assemble.

2. If a project requires "n" components, there will be "n–1" units in stock.

3. A motor will rotate in the wrong direction.

4. A fail-safe circuit will destroy others.

5. A transistor protected by a fast-acting fuse will protect the fuse by blowing first.

6. A failure will not appear till a unit has passed final inspection.

7. A purchased component or instrument will meet its specs long enough, and only long enough, to pass incoming inspection.

8. After the last of sixteen mounting screws has been removed from an access cover, it will be discovered that the wrong access cover has been removed.

9. After an access cover has been secured by sixteen hold-down screws, it will be discovered that the gasket has been omitted.

10. After an instrument has been assembled, extra components will be found on the bench.

## Pattison's Law of Electronics
If wires can be connected in two different ways, the first way blows the fuse.

## Farrell's Law of Newfangled Gadgetry
The most expensive component is the one that breaks.

## The Recommended Practices Committee of the International Society of Philosophical Engineers' Universal Laws for Naive Engineers

1. In any calculation, any error that can creep in will do so.
2. Any error in any calculation will be in the direction of most harm.
3. In any formula, constants (especially those obtained from engineering handbooks) are to be treated as variables.
4. The best approximation of service conditions in the laboratory will not begin to meet those conditions encountered in actual service.
5. The most vital dimension on any plan or drawing stands the greatest chance of being omitted.
6. If only one bid can be secured on any project, the price will be unreasonable.
7. If a test installation functions perfectly, all subsequent production units will malfunction.
8. All delivery promises must be multiplied by a factor of 2.0.
9. Major changes in construction will always be requested after fabrication is nearly completed.
10. Parts that positively cannot be assembled in improper order will be.
11. Interchangeable parts won't.
12. Manufacturer's specifications of performance should be multiplied by a factor of 0.5.

13. Salespeople's claims for performance should be multiplied by a factor of 0.25.

14. Installation and Operating Instructions shipped with the device will be promptly discarded by the Receiving Department.

15. Any device requiring service or adjustment will be least accessible.

16. Service Conditions as given on specifications will be exceeded.

17. If more than one person is responsible for a miscalculation, no one will be at fault.

18. Identical units that test in an identical fashion will not behave in an identical fashion in the field.

19. If, in engineering practice, a safety factor is set through service experience at an ultimate value, an ingenious idiot will promptly calculate a method to exceed said safety factor.

20. Warranty and guarantee clauses are voided by payment of the invoice.

## Klipstein's Law of Specification

In specifications, Murphy's Law supersedes Ohm's.

## Mr. Cooper's Law

If you do not understand a particular word in a piece of technical writing, ignore it. The piece will make perfect sense without it.

## Bogovich's Corollary to Mr. Cooper's Law
If the piece makes no sense without the word, it will make no sense with the word.

## Addendum to Murphy's Law
In precise mathematical terms, $1 + 1 = 2$, where "=" is a symbol meaning "seldom if ever."

## Scott's Second Law
When an error has been detected and corrected, it will be found to have been correct in the first place.
### Corollary
After the correction has been found in error, it will be impossible to fit the original quantity back into the equation.

## Tylczak's Probability Postulate
Random events tend to occur in groups.

## Hartz's Uncertainty Principle
Ambiguity is invariant.

## The Snafu Equations
1. Given any problem containing "n" equations, there will always be "n+1" unknowns.
2. An object or bit of information most needed will be the least available.
3. Once you have exhausted all possibilities and fail,

there will be one solution, simple and obvious, highly
visible to everyone else.
4. Badness comes in waves.

## Skinner's Constant (Flannagan's Finagling Factor)
That quantity which, when multiplied by, divided by, added
to, or subtracted from the answer you get, gives you the answer you should have gotten.

## Einstein's Observation
Inasmuch as the mathematical theorems are related to reality, they are not sure; inasmuch as they are sure, they are not
related to reality.

## Finman's Law of Mathematics
Nobody wants to read anyone else's formulas.

## Von Neumann's Observation
In mathematics you don't understand things. You just get
used to them.

## Golomb's Don'ts of Mathematical Modeling
1. Don't believe the thirty-third-order consequences of
   a first-order model.
   CATCHPHRASE "Cum grano salis."
2. Don't extrapolate beyond the region of fit.
   CATCHPHRASE "Don't go off the deep end."
3. Don't apply any model until you understand the sim-

plifying assumptions on which it is based, and can test their applicability.

CATCHPHRASE "Use only as directed."

4. Don't believe that the model is the reality.

CATCHPHRASE "Don't eat the menu."

5. Don't distort reality to fit the model.

CATCHPHRASE "The 'Procrustes Method.' "

6. Don't limit yourself to a single model. More than one may be useful for understanding different aspects of the same phenomenon.

CATCHPHRASE "Legalize polygamy."

7. Don't retain a discredited model.

CATCHPHRASE "Don't beat a dead horse."

8. Don't fall in love with your model.

CATCHPHRASE "Pygmalion."

9. Don't apply the terminology of Subject A to the problems of Subject B if it is to the enrichment of neither.

CATCHPHRASE "New names for old."

10. Don't expect that by having named a demon you have destroyed him.

CATCHPHRASE "Rumpelstiltskin."

## Einstein on Math and Science

1. The whole of science is nothing more than a refinement of everyday thinking.

2. Technological progress is like an ax in the hands of a pathological criminal.

3. We can't solve problems by using the same kind of thinking we used when we created them.

4. If $A$ is a success in life, then $A$ equals $x$ plus $y$ plus $z$. Work is $x$; $y$ is play; and $z$ is keeping your mouth shut.

5. As far as the laws of mathematics refer to reality, they are not certain; as far as they are certain, they do not refer to reality.

6. Two things are infinite, the universe and human stupidity; and I'm not sure about the universe.

## Walder's Observation
A mathematician is one who is willing to assume everything except responsibility.

## Albinak's Algorithm
When graphing a function, the width of the line should be inversely proportional to the precision of the data.

## First Rule of Applied Mathematics
98% of all statistics are made up.

# mAChiNESmA NSHIP

**Willoughby's Law**
When you try to prove to someone that a machine won't work, it will.

**Washlesky's Law**
Anything is easier to take apart than to put together.

**Rudnicki's Rule**
That which cannot be taken apart will fall apart.

**Rap's Law of Inanimate Reproduction**
If you take something apart and put it back together enough times, eventually you will have two of them.

## Anthony's Law of the Workshop
Any tool, when dropped, will roll into the least accessible corner of the workshop.
*Corollary*
On the way to the corner, any dropped tool will first always strike your toes.

## The Spare Parts Principle
The accessibility, during recovery of small parts that fall from the workbench, varies directly with the size of the part—and inversely with its importance to the completion of work under way.

## Four Workshop Principles
1. The one wrench or drill bit you need will be the one missing from the tool chest.
2. Most projects require three hands.
3. Leftover nuts never match leftover bolts.
4. The more carefully you plan a project, the more confusion there is when something goes wrong.

## Ray's Rule for Precision
Measure with a micrometer.
Mark with chalk.
Cut with an ax.

## Law of Repair
You can't fix it if it ain't broke.

## Rule of Intelligent Tinkering
Save all the parts.

## Johnson's Law
When any mechanical contrivance fails, it will do so at the most inconvenient possible time.

## Laws of Annoyance
When working on a project, if you put away a tool that you're certain you're finished with, you will need it instantly.

## Watson's Law
The reliability of machinery is inversely proportional to the number and significance of any persons watching it.

## Wyszkowski's Law
Anything can be made to work if you fiddle with it long enough.

## Sattinger's Law
It works better if you plug it in.

## Lowery's Law
If it jams—force it. If it breaks, it needed replacing anyway.

## Schmidt's Law
If you mess with a thing long enough, it'll break.

**Fudd's Law of Opposition**
Push something hard enough and it will fall over.

**Anthony's Law of Force**
Don't force it; get a larger hammer.

**O'Rourke's Rule**
Never fight an inanimate object.

**Ralph's Observation**
It is a mistake to allow any mechanical object to realize that you are in a hurry.

**Cahn's Axiom**
When all else fails, read the instructions.

**The Principle Concerning Multifunctional Devices**
The fewer functions any device is required to perform, the more perfectly it can perform those functions.

**The Betamax Principle**
If there are two competing and incompatible technologies on the market, the inferior technology will prevail.

**Lee's Law of Electrical Repair**
The simpler it looks, the more problems it hides.

## Rives's Rule
Everything falls apart on the same day.

## Kagel's Law
Anything adjustable will eventually need adjustment.

## Morris's Assembly Paradox
If you put it together correctly the first time, there was something you should have done before you put it together.

# CyBER-mURPHology

**Law of Unreliability**
To err is human, but to really foul things up requires a computer.

**Greer's Law**
A computer program does what you tell it to do, not what you want it to do.

**Crayne's Law**
All computers wait at the same speed.

**Horowitz's Rule**
A computer makes as many mistakes in two seconds as twenty men working twenty years.

**Robbins's Rule**
One good reason why computers can do more work than people is that they never have to stop and answer the phone.

**Belinda's Law**
The chance of a computer crash is directly proportional to the importance of the document that you are working on.

**Harris's Warning**
The real danger is not that computers will begin to think like men, but that men will begin to think like computers.

**Junior's Law**
Computers make very fast, very accurate mistakes.

**Minsky's Maxim**
No computer has ever been designed that is ever aware of what it's doing, but most of the time, we aren't either.

**Breznikar's Law of Computer Technology**
Applying computer technology is simply finding the right wrench to pound in the correct screw.

**Thompson's Steady State Theory**
The steady state of disks is full.

## The Upgrade Principle

The upgrade will break down as soon as the old version is deleted.

*Corollary*

The old version will not reinstall.

## The Virus Factor

The one file you don't scan for viruses will be the one with the virus.

## Cromer's Law

A digital readout provides misinformation with greater accuracy than previously possible.

## The Third Law of Printing

Immediately after you walk away from the printer, the paper will jam.

## Bradley's Bromide

If computers get too powerful, we can organize them into a committee—that will do them in.

## Murphy's Computers Laws

1. No matter how many resources you have, it is never enough.
2. If a program actually fits in memory and has enough disk space, it is guaranteed to crash.
3. If such a program has not crashed yet, it is waiting for a critical moment before it crashes.

4. All components become obsolete.
5. The speed with which components become obsolete is directly proportional to the price of the component.
6. Software bugs are impossible to detect by anybody except the end user.

## Moore's Law (simplified)
Computer power doubles and prices halve every eighteen months.

## J. T.'s Law of Technical Support
The better the customer service, the sooner you get to speak with someone who can't help you.

## The Programmer's Dilemma
Programming is like sex. One mistake and you're providing support for a lifetime.

## Eighth Law of Programming
It is easier to change the specification to fit the program than vice versa.

## Principle of Operating Systems
Computers are an intelligence sink; there is no level of genius that cannot find its match in system design.

### The Microsoft Corollary
It takes hundreds of geniuses to make a complex thing simple.

## Schyer's Law of Relativity for Programmers
If the code and the comments disagree, then both are probably wrong.

## Perlis's Postulate
The computing field is always in need of new clichés.

## Liz's Law
If you spend hours trying to sign on to a busy server, your connection will be lost as soon as you get on.

## Holten's Download Principle
The likelihood of receiving an error message during a download increases the closer you come to finishing.

## The Download Factor
If a file takes an hour to download, someone in your house will pick up the phone in the fifty-ninth minute.

## Hitch's Internet Law
When connecting to a Web site your request will take the most indirect possible route.

## Reichart's Internet Law
The link button you want to press is the last one that loads.

## Petzen's Internet Law

The most promising result from a search engine query will lead to a dead link.

## McMahon's Rule

No matter what you search for, at least one porn site match your criteria.

## Reasner's Law of the Internet

The probability of your browser locking up is directly proportional to how close you are to the information that you've been searching for.

## Montgomery's Law of the 404 Error

The more you need a particular Web site, the more likely it no longer exists on the server.

## Schaaf's Law of On-Line Research

Any quote found twice on the Internet will have two different wordings, attributions, or both.

*Corollary*

If the wording and source are consistent in two places, they are both wrong.

## Knowles's Laws

1. The number of bogus selections returned on a search increases exponentially with the urgency of your search.
2. Proper use of language declines as technology advances.

## Law of E-Mail
Typos are not noticed until after the "send" button has been hit.

## Sullivan's Lemma
Artificial intelligence is no match for natural stupidity.

## Sutin's Law
The most useless computer tasks are the most fun to do.

## McCristy's Computer Axioms
1. Backup files are never complete.
2. Software bugs are correctable only after the software is judged obsolete by the industry.

## Leo Beiser's Computer Axiom
When putting it into memory, remember where you put it.

## Steinbach's Guideline for Systems Programming
Never test for an error condition you don't know how to handle.

## Troutman's Programming Postulates
1. If a test installation functions perfectly, all subsequent systems will malfunction.
2. Not until a program has been in production for at least six months will the most harmful error be discovered.
3. Profanity is the one language all programmers know best.

## Gilb's Laws of Unreliability

1. Computers are unreliable, but humans are even more unreliable.
2. Any system that depends on human reliability is unreliable.
3. Undetectable errors are infinite in variety, in contrast to detectable errors, which by definition are limited.
4. Investment in reliability will increase until it exceeds the probable cost of errors, or until someone insists on getting some useful work done.

## Murphy's Laws of Techonology

1. Logic is a systematic method of coming to the wrong conclusion with confidence.
2. The attention span of a computer is only as long as its electrical cord.
3. The degree of technical competence is inversely proportional to the level of management.

## McAuley's Axiom

If a system is of sufficient complexity, it will be built before it is designed, implemented before it is tested, and outdated before it is debugged.

## Brook's Law

Adding manpower to a late software project makes it later.

## Laws of Computerdom According to Golub

1. Fuzzy project objectives are used to avoid the embarrassment of estimating the corresponding costs.
2. A carelessly planned project takes three times longer to complete than expected; a carefully planned project takes only twice as long.
3. The effort required to correct course increases geometrically with time.
4. Project teams detest weekly progress reporting because it so vividly manifests their lack of progress.

## Smith's Law of Computer Repair

Access holes will be half an inch too small.

### Corollary

Holes that are the right size will be in the wrong place.

## Murphy's Computer System Definitions

HARDWARE—The parts of a computer system that can be kicked.

SOFTWARE—The parts of a computer system that don't work.

HARD DISK—The part of a computer system that freezes up at the worst possible time.

PERIPHERALS—The parts that are incompatible with your computer system.

PRINTER—The part of the computer system that jams when you're not looking.

CABLE—The part of the computer system that is too short.

MOUSE—See *cursing*.

BACKUP—An operation that is never performed on time.

RESTORE—A procedure that works perfectly until it is needed.

MEMORY—The part of a computer system that is insufficient.

ERROR MESSAGE—A request to okay the destruction of your own data.

FILE—The part of the computer system that cannot be found.

PROCESSOR—The part of a computer system that is obsolete.

MANUAL—The element of your computer system that is incomprehensible.

## The Stages of Systems Development
1. Wild enthusiasm
2. Disillusionment
3. Total confusion
4. Search for the guilty
5. Punishment of the innocent
6. Promotion of the nonparticipants

## Arnold's Laws of Documentation
1. If it should exist, it doesn't.
2. If it does exist, it's out-of-date.
3. Only useless documentation transcends the first two laws.

## Jaruk's Law

If it would be cheaper to buy a new unit, the company will insist upon repairing the old one.

### Corollary

If it would be cheaper to repair the old one, the company will insist on the latest model.

## Picasso's Postulate

Computers are useless. All they give you is answers.

## Osburn's Axiom

Computers are not intelligent. They only think they are.

## Throop's Axiom

The universe is not user-friendly.

## Lubarsky's Law of Cybernetic Entomology

There's always one more bug.

# StaTESMANship

**Lieberman's Law**
Everybody lies, but it doesn't matter since nobody listens.

**Law of the Lie**
No matter how often a lie is shown to be false, there will remain a percentage of people who believe it true.

**The Sausage Principle**
People who love sausage and respect the law should never watch either one being made.

**Jacquin's Postulate on Democratic Government**
No person's life, liberty, or property is safe while the legislature is in session.

**Law of Legislative Action**
The length of time it takes a bill to pass through the legislature is in inverse proportion to the number of lobbying groups favoring it.

**Todd's Two Political Principles**
1. No matter what they're telling you, they're not telling you the whole truth.
2. No matter what they're talking about, they're talking about money.

**The Watergate Principle**
Government corruption is always reported in the past tense.

**Katz's Law**
Men and nations will act rationally when all other possibilities have been exhausted.

**Eldridge's Law of War**
Man is always ready to die for an idea, provided that the idea is not quite clear to him.

**Parker's Law of Political Statements**
The truth of any proposition has nothing to do with its credibility and vice versa.

**Rule of Political Promises**
Truth varies.

## Lee's Law

In any dealings with a collective body of people, the people will always be more tacky than originally expected.

## Evan's Law

If you can keep your head when all about you are losing theirs, then you just don't understand the problem.

## Andra's Political Postulate

Foundation of a party signals the dissolution of the movement.

## Oak's Principles of Lawmaking

1. Law expands in proportion to the resources available for its enforcement.
2. Bad law is more likely to be supplemented than repealed.
3. Social legislation cannot repeal physical laws.

## The Guppy Law

When outrageous expenditures are divided finely enough, the public will not have enough stake in any one expenditure to squelch it.

### *Corollary*

Enough guppies can eat a treasury.

## Wiker's Law

Government expands to absorb revenue and then some.

## Good's Rule for Dealing with Bureaucracies
When the government bureau's remedies do not match your problem, you modify the problem, not the remedy.

## Brown's Rules of Leadership
1. To succeed in politics, it is often necessary to rise above your principles.
2. The best way to succeed in politics is to find a crowd that's going somewhere and get in front of them.

## The Rule of Law
If the facts are against you, argue the law.
If the law is against you, argue the facts.
If the facts and the law are against you, yell like hell.

## Miles's Law
Where you stand depends on where you sit.

## Fibley's Extension to Miles's Law
Where you sit depends on who you know.

## Walton's Law of Politics
A fool and his money are soon elected.

## The Fifth Rule of Politics
When a politician gets an idea, he usually gets it wrong.

**Wilkie's Law**
A good slogan can stop analysis for fifty years.

**First Law of Politics**
Stay in with the outs.

**Robbins's Mini-Max Rule of Government**
Any minimum criteria set will be the maximum value used.

**Lowe's Law**
Success always occurs in private, and failure in full public view.

**Marshall's First Law of the Legislature**
Never let the facts get in the way of a carefully thought-out bad decision.

**France's Rule of Folly**
If a million people believe a foolish thing, it is still a foolish thing.

**Santayana's Observation**
Fanaticism consists of redoubling your efforts when you have forgotten your aim.

**Calvin Coolidge's Comment**
You don't have to explain something you never said.

### Adler's Rule
It is easier to fight for one's principles than to live up to them.

### Main's Law
For every action there is an equal and opposite government program.

### Booker T. Washington's Rule
You can't hold a man down without staying down with him.

### Armey's Axiom
You can't get ahead while getting even.

### L.B.J.'s Law
If two people agree on everything, you may be sure that one of them is doing the thinking.

### Heine's Law
One should forgive one's enemies, but not before they are hanged.

### Ameringer's Axiom
Politics is the gentle art of getting votes from the poor and campaign funds from the rich by promising to protect each from the other.

### Thomas Jefferson's Rule
Delay is preferable to error.

## The Oil Spill Principle

People will accept any bad news if the magnitude of the disaster is revealed gradually.

## Sherman's Rule of Press Conferences

The explanation of a disaster will be made by a stand-in.

## Lovka's First Political Principle

There is no sincerity like a politician telling a lie.

## Cameron's Law

An honest politician is one who, when he is bought, will stay bought.

## Duck's Political Principle

Any campaign reform only lasts until the powers regroup.

## Perot's Observation

The only thing most politicians stand for is reelection.

## Nowlan's Law

Following the path of least resistance is what makes politicians and rivers crooked.

## Shaffer's Law

The effectiveness of a politician varies in inverse proportion to his commitment to principle.

### Hunter's Law
No matter how dishonorable, every politician considers himself honorable.

### Wilson's Law of Politics
If you want to make enemies, try to change something.

### Evan's Law
Once you give up integrity, the rest is easy.

### Abourezk's Laws of Politics
1. Don't worry about your enemies. It's your allies who will do you in.
2. The bigger the appropriations bill, the shorter the debate.
3. If you want to curry favor with a politician, give him credit for something that someone else did.

### Political Pollster's Rules
1. When the polls are in your favor, flaunt them.
2. When the polls are overwhelmingly unfavorable, (a) ridicule and dismiss them; or (b) stress the volatility of public opinion.
3. When the polls are slightly unfavorable, play for sympathy as a struggling underdog.
4. When too close to call, be surprised at your own strength.

### Lawrence's Law
A diplomat is someone who can tell you to go to hell in such a way that you will look forward to the trip.

### Podnos's Law
One is tolerant only of that which does not concern him.

### Syrus's Leadership Principle
Anyone can hold the helm when the sea is calm.

### Primary Political Corollary
A good slogan beats a good solution.

### Galbraith's Law of Politics
Anyone who says he isn't going to resign, four times, definitely will.

### Law of Governmental Self-Fulfillment
The more money spent on the feasibility study, the more feasible the project.

### Kamin's Law
When attempting to predict and forecast macroeconomic moves of economic legislation by a politician, never be misled by what he says; instead—watch what he does.

## Inge's Axiom
It is useless for sheep to pass resolutions in favor of vegetarianism while wolves remain of a different opinion.

## Shaw's Political Principle
A government that robs Peter to pay Paul can always depend on the support of Paul.

## The Rule of Law
Never make a major policy change based on a close vote.

## Potter's Law
A rumor doesn't gain credence until it's officially denied.

## Napolean's Observation
Rascality has limits; stupidity has not.

# ECoNO-mURPHology

### Horngren's Observation
Among economists, the real world is often a special case.

### Marks's Law of Monetary Equalization
A fool and your money are soon partners.

### Heisenberg Principle of Investment
You may know where the market is going, but you can't possibly know where it's going after that.

### Jeff's Theory of the Stock Market
The price of a stock moves inversely to the number of shares purchased.

### Miller's Law
Exceptions prove the rule—and wreck the budget.

**Buckwald's Law**
As the economy gets better, everything else gets worse.

**De Balzak's Axiom**
Behind every great fortune, there is a crime.

**Thurber's Law**
There is no safety in numbers, or in anything else.

**Wingfield's Axiom**
Accuracy is the sum total of your compensating mistakes.

**Crane's Law**
There ain't no such thing as a free lunch.

**Charles Osgood's Axiom**
Nobody thinks they make too much money.

**Cade's Law of Budgeting**
The larger the budget, the less effectively the funds are allocated.

**The Budgetary Reminder**
A budget is just a method of worrying before you spend money as well as afterward.

**Glynn's Law**
The amount of aggravation inherent in a business transaction is inversely proportional to the profit.

# ACaDeMIology

**H. L. Mencken's Law**
Those who can, do.
Those who cannot, teach.
*Martin's Extension*
Those who cannot teach, administrate.

**Meredith's Law for Grad School Survival**
Never let your major professor know that you exist.

**Vile's Law for Educators**
No one is listening until you make a mistake.

**Seeger's Law**
Anything in parentheses can be ignored.

## Vile's Law of Grading Papers
All papers after the top are upside down or backward, until you right the pile. Then the process repeats.

## Weiner's Law of Libraries
There are no answers, only cross-references.

## Laws of Class Scheduling
1. If the course you wanted most has room for "n" students, you will be the "n+1" to apply.
2. Class schedules are designed so that every student will waste maximum time between classes.

*Corollary*

When you are occasionally able to schedule two classes in a row, they will be held in classrooms at opposite ends of the campus.

3. A prerequisite for a desired course will be offered only during the semester following the desired course.

## First Law of Final Exams
Pocket calculator batteries that have lasted all semester will fail during the math final.

*Corollary*

If you bring extra batteries, they will be defective.

## Second Law of Final Exams
In your toughest final, the most distractingly attractive student in class will sit next to you for the first time.

## Laws of Applied Terror

1. When reviewing your notes before an exam, the most important ones will be illegible.
2. The more studying you did for the exam, the less sure you are as to which answer they want.
3. Eighty percent of the final exam will be based on the one lecture you missed about the book you didn't read.
4. The night before the English history midterm, your biology instructor will assign two hundred pages on planaria.

*Corollary*

Every instructor assumes that you have nothing else to do except study for that instructor's course.

5. If you are given an open-book exam, you will forget your book.

*Corollary*

If you are given a take-home exam, you will forget where you live.

6. At the end of the semester you will recall having enrolled in a course at the beginning of the semester—and never attending.

## Natalie's Law of Algebra

You never catch on until after the test.

## Seit's Law of Higher Education

The one course you must take to graduate will not be offered during your last semester.

## Murphy's Rule of the Term Paper

The book or periodical most vital to the completion of your term paper will be missing from the library.

*Corollary*

If it is available, the most important page will be torn out.

## Duggan's Law of Scholarly Research

The most valuable quotation will be the one for which you cannot determine the source.

*Corollary*

The source for an unattributed quotation will appear in the most hostile review of your work.

## Rominger's Rules for Teachers

1. When a student asks for a second time if you have read his book report, he did not read the book.
2. If daily class attendance is mandatory, a scheduled exam will produce increased absenteeism. If attendance is optional, a scheduled exam will produce persons you have never seen before.

## Darrow's Comment on History

History repeats itself. That's one of the things wrong with history.

## Primary Rule of History

History doesn't repeat itself—historians merely repeat each other.

## Coleman's Commentary on Santayana
Those who fail to learn from the past are condemned to repeat history class.

## Valery's Law
History is the science of what never happens twice.

## Prescher's Law of Exams
If you don't know the answer, someone will ask the question.

## The Student's Tautology
The teacher is never absent on the day of the exam.

## Herrnstein's Law
The attention paid to an instructor is a constant regardless of the size of the class; thus, as the class swells, the amount of attention paid per student drops in direct ratio.

## Kissinger's Axiom
University politics are vicious precisely because the stakes are so small.

## Plutarch's Rule
It is impossible for anyone to learn that which he thinks he already knows.

# WoRKMANship

**Lofta's Lament**
Nobody can leave well enough alone.

**Hardin's Law**
You can never do just one thing.

**Ziggy's Law**
Do a little more each day than everyone expects and soon everyone will expect more.

**Harrison's Postulate**
For every action, there is an equal and opposite criticism.

**Shand's Law**
The more efficiently a project is done, the greater the chance it will have to be undone.

**Edison's Observation**
Opportunity is missed by most people because it is dressed in overalls and looks like work.

**Hecht's Law**
There no time like the present for postponing what you don't want to do.

**Grossman's Lemma**
Any task worth doing was worth doing yesterday.

**Dehay's Axiom**
Simple jobs always get put off because there will be time to do them later.

**Parkinson's First Law**
Work expands to fill the time available for its completion; the thing to be done swells in perceived importance and complexity in a direct ratio with the time to be spent in its completion.

**Parkinson's Second Law**
Expenditures rise to meet income.

## The Einstein Extension of Parkinson's Law

A work project expands to fill the space available.

*Corollary*

No matter how large the workspace, if two projects must be done at the same time they will require the use of the same part of the workspace.

## Laws of Applied Confusion

1. The one piece that the plant forgot to ship is the one that supports 75 percent of the balance of the shipment.

*Corollary*

   Not only did the plant forget to ship it, 50 percent of the time they haven't even made it.

2. Truck deliveries that normally take one day will take five when you are waiting for the truck.

3. After adding two weeks to the schedule for unexpected delays, add two more for the unexpected, unexpected delays.

4. In any structure, pick out the one piece that should not be mismarked and expect the plant to cross you up.

*Corollaries*

1. In any group of pieces with the same erection mark on it, one should not have that mark on it.

2. It will not be discovered until you try to put it where the mark says it's supposed to go.

3. Never argue with the fabricating plant about an error. The inspection prints are all checked off, even to the holes that aren't there.

**Hoffstedt's Employment Principle**
Confusion creates jobs.

**Wyszkowski's Theorem**
Regardless of the units used by either the supplier or the customer, the manufacturer shall use their own arbitrary units convertible to those of either the supplier or the customer only by means of weird and unnatural conversion factors.

**Byrne's Law of Concreting**
When you pour, it rains.

**Bowersox's Law of the Workshop**
If you have only one nail, it will bend.

**Second Law of the Workshop**
You can always find three nuts to fit the four screws you need.

**The Extra-Part Principle**
You never know what that extra part is for until you've thrown it away.

**Coull's Comment**
Every new project requires a tool that you don't have.

## Thoreau's Observation

Men have become the tools of their tools.

## The Machine Rules

1. Nothing will work that is put back together in the reverse of the way it was dismantled.
2. The last turn on any nut or bolt will strip it or snap it off.

### Corollary

Without the last turn, the nut or bolt will fall off.

## Law of Product Testing

A component selected at random from a group having 99 percent reliability, will be a member of the 1 percent group.

## Campbell's Maxim

Hell is the place where everything tests perfectly and nothing works.

# OffICE mURPHology

**Six Laws of Office Murphology**

1. Important letters that contain no errors will develop errors in the mail.

*Corollary*

Corresponding errors will show up in the duplicate while the boss is reading it.

2. Office machines that function perfectly during normal business hours will break down when you return to the office at night to use them for personal business.

3. Machines that have broken down will work perfectly when the person who repairs them arrives.

4. Envelopes and stamps that don't stick when you lick them will stick to other things when you don't want them to.

5. Vital papers will demonstrate their vitality by sponta-

neously moving from where you left them to where you can't find them.

6. The last person who quit or was fired will be held responsible for everything that goes wrong—until the next person quits or is fired.

## Devries's Dilemma
If you hit two keys on the typewriter, the one you don't want hits the paper.

## Theory of Selective Supervision
The one time in the day that you lean back and relax is the one time the boss walks through the office.

## Launegayer's Observation
Asking dumb questions is easier than correcting dumb mistakes.

## Bogovich's Law
He who hesitates is probably right.

## Strano's Law
When all else fails, try the boss's suggestion.

## Brintnall's Law
If you are given two contradictory orders, obey them both.

## Shapiro's Law of Reward
The one who does the least work will get the most credit.

## Laws of Procrastination
1. Procrastination shortens the job and places the responsibility for its termination on someone else (the authority who imposed the deadline).
2. It reduces anxiety by reducing the expected quality of the project from the best of all possible efforts to the best that can be expected given the limited time.
3. Status is gained in the eyes of others, and in one's own eyes, because it is assumed that the importance of the work justifies the stress.
4. Avoidance of interruptions including the assignment of other duties can usually be achieved so that the obviously stressed worker can concentrate on the single effort.
5. Procrastination avoids boredom; one never has the feeling that there is nothing important to do.
6. It may eliminate the job if the need passes before the job can be done.

## Doane's Laws of Procrastination
1. The more proficient one is at procrastination, the less proficient one need be at all else.
2. The slower one works, the fewer mistakes one makes.

## Jeff's Law of Procrastination
Hard work has a future payoff. Laziness pays off now.

## Hampton's Homily
The trouble with doing something right the first time is that nobody appreciates how difficult it was.

## Murphy's Law of Punctuality
Being punctual means only that your mistake will be made on time.

## Quile's Consultation Law
The job that pays the most will be offered when there is no time to deliver the services.

## Johnson's Law
The number of minor illnesses among the employees is inversely proportional to the health of the organization.

## Tillis's Organizational Principle
If you file it, you'll know where it is but never need it.
If you don't file it, you'll need it but never know where it is.

## Sandiland's Law
Free time that unexpectedly becomes available will be wasted.

## Scott's Law of Business
Never walk down a hallway in an office building without a piece of paper in your hand.

## Table of Handy Office Excuses
1. That's the way we've always done it.
2. I didn't know you were in a hurry for it.
3. No one told me to go ahead.
4. I'm waiting for an okay.
5. How did I know this was different?
6. That's his job, not mine.
7. Wait till the boss comes back and ask him.
8. We don't make many mistakes.
9. I didn't think it was very important.
10. I'm so busy, I just can't get around to it.
11. I thought I told you.
12. I wasn't hired to do that.

## Drummond's Law of Personnel Recruiting
The ideal résumé will turn up one day after the position is filled.

## Dedera's Law
In a three-story building served by one elevator, nine times out of ten the elevator car will be on a floor where you are not.

## Gluck's Law
Whichever way you turn upon entering an elevator, the buttons will be on the opposite side.

### Lynch's Law
The elevator always comes after you have put down your bag.

### Cafeteria Law
The item you had your eye on the minute you walked in will be taken by the person in front of you.

### Rush's Rule of Gravity
When you drop change at a vending machine, the pennies will fall nearby while the other coins will roll out of sight.

### Pinto's Law
Do someone a favor and it becomes your job.

### Connor's Law
If something is confidential, it will be left in the copier machine.

### Kranske's Law
Beware of a day during which you don't have something to bitch about.

### Langsam's Ornithological Axiom
It's difficult to soar with eagles when you work with turkeys.

# SoCIO-mURPHology

**Shirley's Law**
Most people deserve each other.

**Harris's Lament**
All the good ones are taken.

**Arthur's Laws of Love**
1. People to whom you are attracted invariably think you remind them of someone else.
2. The love letter you finally got the courage to send will be delayed in the mail long enough for you to make a fool of yourself in person.
3. Other people's romantic gestures seem novel and exciting. Your own romantic gestures seem foolish and clumsy.

## Thoms's Law of Marital Bliss
The length of a marriage is inversely proportional to the amount spent on the wedding.

## O'Reilly's Observation
It's not love that lasts forever, it's plastic.

## Murphy's First Law for Husbands
The first time you go out after your wife's birthday you will see the gift you gave her marked down 50 percent.
### Corollary
If she is with you, she will assume you chose it because it was cheap.

## Murphy's Second Law for Husbands
The gifts you buy your wife are never as apropos as the gifts your neighbor buys his wife.

## Angela's Axiom
The last sheet of gift wrap will be six inches smaller than the last gift to wrap.

## Bedfellow's Rule
The one who snores will fall asleep first.

## Farmer's Credo
Sow your wild oats on Saturday night—then on Sunday pray for crop failure.

**Ruby's Principle of Close Encounters**
The probability of meeting someone you know increases when you are with someone you don't want to be seen with.

**Cheit's Lament**
If you help a friend in need, he is sure to remember you—the next time he's in need.

**Johnson's Law**
If, in the course of several months, only three worthwhile social events take place, they will all fall on the same evening.

**Denniston's Law**
Virtue is its own punishment.

**Mason's Law of Synergism**
The one day you'd sell your soul for something, souls are a glut.

**Jan and Martha's Law of the Beauty Shop**
The most flattering comments on your hair come the day before you're scheduled to have it cut.

**Jilly's Law**
The worse the haircut, the slower it grows out.

**Reynold's Law of Climatology**
Wind velocity increases directly with the cost of the hairdo.

### Reverend Chichester's Laws

1. If the weather is extremely bad, church attendance will be down.
2. If the weather is extremely good, church attendance will be down.
3. If the church bulletins are in short supply, church attendance will exceed all expectations.

### Weatherwax's Postulate

The degree to which you overreact to information will be in inverse proportion to its accuracy.

### The Law of the Letter

The best way to inspire fresh thoughts is to seal the letter.

### Milstead's Christmas Card Rule

After you have mailed your last card, you will receive a card from someone you overlooked.

### Laws of Postal Delivery

1. Love letters, business contracts, and money you are due always arrive three weeks late.
2. Junk mail arrives the day it was sent.

### McLaughlin's Law

In a key position in every genealogy you will find a John Smith from London.

## The Whispered Rule
People will believe anything if you whisper it.

## The Mosquito Principle
When two people are together outdoors, the insects will bother one while leaving the other alone.

## Ron's Observations for Teenagers
1. The pimples don't appear until the hour before the date.
2. The scratch on the CD is always through the song you like most.

## Johnson and Laird's Law
A toothache tends to start on Saturday night.

## Schrimpton's Law of Teenage Opportunity
When opportunity knocks, you've got headphones on.

## Underlying Principle of Sociogenetics
Superiority is recessive.

## Dooley's Law
Trust everybody, but cut the cards.

## Meader's Law
Whatever happens to you, it will previously have happened to everyone you know.

## Bocklage's Law
He who laughs last probably didn't get the joke.

## First Law of Sociogenetics
Celibacy is not hereditary.

## Farber's Law
Necessity is the mother of strange bedfellows.

## Hartley's Law
Never sleep with anyone crazier than yourself.

## Beckhap's Law
Beauty times brains equals a constant.

## Pardo's Postulate
Anything good in life is either illegal, immoral, or fattening.

## Parker's Law
Beauty is only skin-deep, but ugly goes clean to the bone.

## Captain Penny's Law
You can fool all of the people some of the time, and some of the people all of the time, but you can't fool MOM.

## Mr. Cole's Axiom
The sum of the intelligence on the planet remains a constant; the population, however, continues to grow.

## Steele's Plagiarism of Somebody's Philosophy
Everybody should believe in something—I believe I'll have another drink.

## The Kennedy Constant
Don't get mad—get even.

## Jones's Motto
Friends come and go, but enemies accumulate.

## McClaughry's Codicil to Jones's Motto
To make an enemy, do someone a favor.

## Munder's Theorem
For every "10" there are ten "1s."

## Cohen's Law
People are divided into two groups—the righteous and the unrighteous—and the righteous do the dividing.

## The Ire Principle
Never try to pacify anyone at the height of their rage.

## Kent Family Law
Never change your plans because of the weather.

## Law of Arrival
Those who live closest arrive latest.

## The Three Least Credible
## Sentences in the English Language

1. "The check is in the mail."
2. "Of course I'll respect you in the morning."
3. "I'm from the government and I'm here to help you."

## Voltaire's Law

There is nothing more respectable than an ancient evil.

## Berra's Law

Anyone who is popular is bound to be disliked.

## Beirce's Definition

A boor is a person who talks when you wish him to listen.

## A Twain Observation

Good breeding consists of concealing how much we think of ourselves and how little we think of the other person.

## Law of Aspersion

If you say something bad about someone, you will discover that the same criticism applies to you.

### Corollary

The only faults that bother us in others are faults we share.

## Goldstick's Rule

Be kind to everyone you talk with. You never know who's going to be on the jury.

## Murphy's First Law of Dieting
The first pounds you lose are in areas in which you didn't want to lose them.

## Keller's Constant
Any flattering photo of yourself will, at some point, elicit a comment that the photo looks nothing like you.

## Lovka's Other Advice
Never rely on a person who uses "party" as a verb.

## Onassis's Axiom
If women didn't exist, all the money in the world would have no meaning.

## Norman's Law
No man knows what true happiness is until he gets married. By then, of course, it's too late.

## Tristan's Law
Appealingness is inversely proportional to attainability.

## Yasenek's Observation
Kissing is a means of getting two people so close together that they can't see anything wrong with each other.

## Tom's Law
When you finally meet the perfect woman, she will be waiting for the perfect man.

## The Feminist Dictum
A woman without a man is like a fish without a bicycle.

## Friedman's Response to the Feminist Dictum
A man without a woman is like a neck without a pain.

## Sarah's Law
You never begin your summer romance until the last day of summer.

## The Puritan Principle
If it feels good, don't do it.

## Liz Taylor's Observation
The problem with people who have no vices is that generally you can be pretty sure they're going to have some pretty annoying virtues.

## Logan's Lament
Even the best of friends cannot attend each other's funeral.

# HoUSEHoLD mURPHology

**Gillette's Law of Telephone Dynamics**

The phone call you've been waiting for comes the minute you're out the door.

**Frank's Phone Phenomena**

If you have a pen, there's no paper.
If you have paper, there's no pen.
If you have both, there's no message.

**Imbesi's Law of the Conservation of Filth**

In order for something to become clean, something else must become dirty.

*Freeman's Extension*

But you can get everything dirty without getting anything clean.

## The VCR Rule
The most expensive special feature on the VCR never gets used.

## Sir Walter's Law
The tendency of smoke from a cigarette, barbecue, campfire, etc. to drift into a person's face varies directly with that person's sensitivity to smoke.

## O'Reilly's Law of the Kitchen
Cleanliness is next to impossible.

## Seven Laws of Kitchen Confusion
1. Multiple-function gadgets will not perform any function adequately.

*Corollary*

The more expensive the gadget, the less often you will use it.

2. The simpler the instructions (e.g., "Press here"), the more difficult it will be to open the package.

3. In a family recipe you just discovered in an old book, the most vital measurement will be illegible.

*Corollary*

You will discover that you can't read it only after you have mixed all the other ingredients.

4. Once a dish is fouled up, anything added to save it only makes it worse.

5. You are always complimented on the item that took the least effort to prepare.

*Example*

If you make "duck à l'orange" you will be complimented on the baked potato.

6. The one ingredient you made a special trip to the store to get will be the one thing your guest is allergic to.

7. The more time and energy you put into preparing a meal, the greater the chance your guests will spend the entire meal discussing other meals they have had.

## Hammond's Laws of the Kitchen

1. Soufflés rise and cream whips only for the family and for guests you didn't really want to invite anyway.

2. The rotten egg will be the one you break into the cake batter.

3. Any cooking utensil placed in the dishwasher will be needed immediately thereafter for something else; any measuring utensil used for liquid ingredients will be needed immediately thereafter for dry ingredients.

4. Time spent consuming a meal is in inverse proportion to time spent preparing it.

5. Whatever it is, somebody will have had it for lunch.

## Working Cook's Laws

1. If you're wondering if you took the meat out to thaw, you didn't.

2. If you're wondering if you left the coffeepot plugged in, you did.
3. If you're wondering if you need to stop and pick up bread and eggs on the way home, you do.

## The Party Law
The more food you prepare, the less your guests eat.

## Mrs. Weiler's Law
Anything is edible if it is chopped finely enough.

## Fausner's Rule of the Household
A knife too dull to cut anything else can always cut your finger.

## Hamilton's Rule for Cleaning Glassware
The spot you are scrubbing is always on the other side.
*Corollary*
If the spot is on the inside, you won't be able to reach it.

## Yeager's Law
Washing machines only break down during the wash cycle.
*Corollaries*
1. All breakdowns occur on the plumber's day off.
2. Cost of repair can be determined by multiplying the cost of your new coat by 1.75, or by multiplying the cost of a new washer by .75.

**Walker's Law of the Household**
There is always more dirty laundry than clean laundry.

**Clive's Rebuttal to Walker's Law**
If it's clean, it isn't laundry.

**Skoff's Law**
A child will not spill on a dirty floor.

**Van Roy's Law**
An unbreakable toy is useful for breaking other toys.

**Mom's Law**
A show-off is any child who is more talented than yours.

**The Three Ways to Get Something Done**
1. Do it yourself.
2. Hire someone to do it for you.
3. Forbid your kids to do it.

**F. P. Jones's Observation**
Children are unpredictable. You never know what inconsistency they're going to catch you in next.

**Davis's Dictum**
We can childproof our homes, but they still get in.

## Pulliam's Postulate
Never step in anything soft.

## Cliff's Law
Never stand between a dog and a hydrant.

## The Spare Button Principle
Shirts that come with extra buttons never lose buttons.

## Mrs. Fergus's Observation
The lost sock reappears only after its match has been discarded.

## Law of Opportunity
The only time the world beats a path to your door is when you are in the bathroom.

## The Reja-Jansen Law
On the first pull of the cord, the drapes will move the wrong way.

## H. Fish's Law of Animal Behavior
The probability of a cat eating dinner has absolutely nothing to do with the price of the food placed before it.

## Fiske's Teenage Corollary to Parkinson's Law
The stomach expands to accommodate the amount of junk food available.

## Ballance's Law of Relativity

How long a minute is depends on which side of the bathroom door you're on.

## The Guest Rule

Never mistake endurance for hospitality.

## Austin's Law

Anything tastes better in someone else's house.

## Britt's Green Thumb Postulate

The life expectancy of a houseplant varies inversely with its price and directly with its ugliness.

## Marquette's Laws of Home Repair

1. The tool you need is just out of reach.
2. The first replacement part you buy will be the wrong size.
3. A lost tool will be found immediately upon purchasing a new one.

## Malone's Law of the Household

If you wait all day for the repairman, you'll wait all day. If you go out for five minutes, he'll arrive and leave while you're gone.

## Minton's Law of Painting

Any paint, no matter what the quality or composition, will adhere permanently to any surface if applied accidentally.

## Laws of Gardening

1. Other people's tools work only in other people's gardens.
2. Fancy gizmos don't work.
3. If nobody uses it, there's a reason.
4. You get the most of what you need the least.

## Law of Reruns

If you have watched a TV series only once, and you watch it again, it will be a rerun of the same episode.

## Jones's Law of TV Programming

1. If there are only two shows worth watching, they will be on at the same time.
2. The only new show worth watching will be canceled.
3. The show you've been looking forward to all week will be preempted.

## Bess's Universal Principles

1. The telephone will ring when you are outside the door, fumbling for your keys.
2. You will reach it just in time to hear the click of the caller hanging up.

## Kovac's Conundrum

When you dial a wrong number, you never get a busy signal.

### Bell's Theorem
When a body is immersed in water, the telephone rings.

### Ryan's Application to Parkinson's Law
Possessions increase to fill the space available for their storage.

### Ringwald's Law of Household Geometry
Any horizontal surface is soon piled up.

### The Pineapple Principle
The best parts of anything are always impossible to separate from the worst parts.

### O'Toole's Axiom
One child is not enough, but two children are far too many.

### Diner's Dilemma
A clean tie attracts the soup of the day.

### Thiessen's Law of Gastronomy
The hardness of the butter is in direct proportion to the softness of the roll.

### Woodside's Grocery Principle
The bag that breaks is the one with the eggs.

### Esther's Law
The fussiest person will be the one to get the chipped coffee cup, the glass with lipstick, or the hair in the food.

### Pope's Law
Chipped dishes never break.

### The Pet Principle
No matter which side of the door the dog or cat is on, it is the wrong side.

### Seymour's Investment Principle
Never invest in anything that eats.

### Rule of Feline Frustration
When your cat has fallen asleep on your lap and looks utterly content and adorable, you will suddenly have to go to the bathroom.

### Boren's Law for Cats
When in doubt, wash.

### Horowitz's Law
Whenever you turn on the radio, you hear the last few notes of your favorite song.

## Berkshire's Law of Household Budgeting
Just after you've made both ends meet, someone moves the ends.

## Murphy's Food Laws
1. Everything you enjoy is bad for you.
2. If it isn't bad for you, you can't afford it.
3. If you can afford it, it's out of season.
4. Every recipe includes one ingredient that you do not have in your kitchen.
5. Substitutions never taste right.
6. Ovens either overcook or undercook. Microwave ovens overcook and undercook at the same time.
7. If you don't make a list, you will forget the most important item.
8. If you do make a list, the store will be out of the most important item.
9. Every item in the store will be on sale, except the items that you want.
10. Coupons always expire before you have a chance to use them.

## Langfield's Law of Gastronomy
The discovery of a new dish is more beneficial to humanity than the discovery of a new star.

### Isaac's Strange Rule of Staleness
Any food that starts out hard will soften when stale. Any food that starts out soft will harden when stale.

### Barbara's Law
Never say "wow" with food in your mouth.

### Grown Child's Lament
Mother said there would be days like this, but she never said there would be so many.

# ROaDSMaNShIP

**Snider's Law**
Nothing can be done in one trip.

**Grandpa Charnock's Law**
You never really learn to swear until you learn to drive.

**Law of Life's Highway**
If everything is coming your way, you're in the wrong lane.

**Relativity for Children**
Time moves slower in a fast-moving vehicle.

## Athena's Rules of Driving Courtesy

If you allow someone to get in front of you, either

a) the car in front will be the last one over a railroad crossing, and you will be stuck waiting for a long, slow-moving train; or

b) you both will have the same destination, and the other car will get the last parking space.

## Lemar's Parking Postulate

After you have to park six blocks away, you will find two new parking spaces right in front of the building entrance.

## McKee's Law

When you're not in a hurry, the traffic light will turn green as soon as your vehicle comes to a complete stop.

## Quigley's Law

A car and a truck approaching each other on an otherwise deserted road will meet at the narrow bridge.

## First Law of Traffic

The slow lane you were stopped in starts moving as soon as you leave it.

## Reece's Law

The speed of an oncoming vehicle is directly proportional to the length of the passing zone.

**Miller's Law of Insurance**
Insurance covers everything except what happens.

**Milstead's Driving Principle**
Whenever you need to stop at a light to put on makeup, every light will be green.

**Lovka's Law of Driving**
There is no traffic until you need to make a left turn.

**Drew's Law of Highway Biology**
The first bug to hit a clean windshield lands directly in front of your eyes.

**Gray's Law for Buses**
A bus that has refused to arrive will do so only when the would-be rider has walked to a point so close to the destination that it is no longer worthwhile to board the bus.

**Karinthy's Definition**
A bus is a vehicle that goes on the other side in the opposite direction.

**Rennie's Law of Public Transit**
If you start walking, the bus will come when you are precisely halfway between stops.

### Jean's Law of Automotives
Any car utilized as a "backup" car breaks down just after the primary car breaks down.

### Law of Bicycling
No matter which way you ride, it's uphill and against the wind.

### Humphries's Law of Bicycling
The shortest route has the steepest hills.

### Campbell's Laws of Automotive Repair
1. If you can get to the faulty part, you don't have the tool to get it off.
2. If you can get the part off, the parts house will have it back-ordered.
3. If it's in stock, it didn't need replacing in the first place.

### Bromberg's Laws of Automotive Repair
1. When the need arises, any tool or object closest to you becomes a hammer.
2. No matter how minor the task, you will inevitably end up covered with grease and motor oil.
3. When necessary, metric and inch tools can be used interchangeably.

### Femo's Law of Automotive Engine Repairing
If you drop something, it will never reach the ground.

## Lorenz's Law of Mechanical Repair
After your hands become coated with grease, your nose will begin to itch.

## Firmage's Rule of Auto Repair
That which is attached with only two bolts is directly behind something attached with eight.

## Cusak's Observation
The driver's-side windshield wiper always wears out first.
*Corollary*
The worst smear is at eye level.

## Randall's Law of Automotives
The flat doesn't occur until the day after the tire sale.

## Rob's Lament
As soon as you become familiar with all the shortcuts and secret parking places in town, you will be transferred to a different town.

## Hyman's Highway Hypothesis
The shortest distance between two points is usually under construction.

## Benedict's Law of Carpooling
As soon as you switch to the carpool lane, the other lanes of traffic speed up.

## Grelb's Frightening Thought
Eighty percent of all people consider themselves to be above average drivers.

## Dale's Parking Postulate
If only two cars are left in a parking lot, one will be blocking the other.

## Rita's Rule
The one time you don't put money in the meter will coincide with the one daily visit of the meter maid.

## Jaroslovsky's Law
The distance you have to park from your apartment increases in proportion to the weight of the packages you are carrying.

# TRaVEL mURPHology

**Wolter's Law**
If you have the time, you won't have the money. If you have the money, you won't have the time.

**Parson's Law of Passports**
No one is as ugly as their passport photo.

**Rune's Rule**
If you don't care where you are, you ain't lost.

**Kauffman's Law of Airports**
The distance to the gate is inversely proportional to the time available to catch your flight.

### Rogers's Law
As soon as the stewardess serves the coffee, the airliner encounters turbulence.

### Davis's Explanation of Rogers' Law
Serving coffee on an aircraft causes turbulence.

### Basic Baggage Principle
Whatever carousel you stand by, your baggage will come in on another one.

### Oliver's Law of Location
No matter where you go, there you are!

### First Law of Travel
It always takes longer to get there than to get back.

### The Airplane Law
When the plane you are on is late, the plane you want to transfer to is on time.

### Stitzer's Vacation Principle
When packing for a vacation, take half as much clothing and twice as much money.

### Kelly's Law of Navigation
The most important information on any map is on the fold.

## The Eclipse Principle
The longer you travel to view an eclipse, the greater the chance of cloud cover.

## The Rent-a-Car Law
In any airport served by several car rental agencies, the other service shuttles will arrive before yours.

## Jeff's Law of Rental Cars
When buying gas for a rental car, nine times out of ten you will pull up to the wrong side of the gas pump.

# SPoRTS mURPHology

**Wise Fan's Lament**

Fools rush in—and get the best seats.

**Breda's Rule**

At any event, the people whose seats are farthest from the aisle arrive last.

**Moser's Law of Spectator Sports**

Exciting plays occur only while you are watching the scoreboard or out buying a hot dog.

**Veeck's Law of Baseball**

Knowledge of the game is inversely proportional to the price of the seats.

## Bob's Law of Televised Sports
If you switch from one football game to another in order to avoid a commercial, the second game will be running a commercial, too.

## Jim Murray's Rules of the Arena
1. Nothing is ever so bad it can't be made worse by firing the coach.
2. The wrong quarterback is the one that's in there.
3. A free agent is anything but.
4. Hockey is a game played by six good players and the home team.
5. Whatever can go to New York, will.

## Indisputable Law of Sports Contracts
The more money the free agent signs for, the less effective he is the following season.

## Knox's Principle of Star Quality
Whenever a superstar is traded to your favorite team, he fades. Whenever your team trades away a useless no-name, he immediately rises to stardom.

## McCarthy's Maxim
A football coach has to be smart enough to understand the game but dumb enough to think it's important.

### Hertzberg's Law of Wing Walking
Never leave hold of what you've got until you've got hold of something else.

### Ken's Law
A flying particle will seek the nearest eye.

### Terman's Law of Innovation
If you want a track team to win the high jump, you find one person who can jump seven feet, not seven people who can jump one foot.

### Lavia's Law of Tennis
A mediocre player will sink to the level of the opposition.

### Lefty Gomez's Law
If you don't throw it, they can't hit it.

### Law of Practice
Plays that work in theory do not work in practice.
Plays that work in practice do not work during the game.

### Sigstad's Law
When it gets to be your turn, they change the rules.

### The Poker Principle
Never do card tricks for the group you play poker with.

## Stenderup's Law
The sooner you fall behind, the more time you will have to catch up.

## Wagner's Law of Sports Coverage
When the camera isolates on a male athlete, he will spit, pick, or scratch.

## Dorr's Law of Athletics
In an otherwise empty locker room, any two individuals will have adjoining lockers.

## The Rule of the Rally
The only way to make up for being lost is to make record time while you are lost.

## Porkingham's Laws of Sportfishing
1. The least experienced fisherman always catches the biggest fish.
2. The worse your line is tangled, the better the fishing is around you.

## Michehl's Rule for Prospective Mountain Climbers
The mountain gets steeper as you get closer.
### Frothingham's Corollary
The mountain looks closer than it is.

## Shedenhelm's Law of Backpacking
All trails have more uphill sections than they have level or downhill sections.

## Law of Bridge
It's always the partner's fault.

## Smith's Laws of Bridge
1. If your hand contains a singleton or a void, that is the suit your partner will bid.
2. If your hand contains the K, J, nine of diamonds and the ace of spades, when the dummy is spread to your left it will contain the A, Q, ten of diamonds, and the king of spades.
3. The trump suit never breaks favorably when you are declarer.

## Thomas's Law of Board Games
The one who least wants to play is the one who will win.

## Gilbert's Law of Sports
Wherever you park, your seats will be on the other side of the stadium.

## Anton's Law of Stadiums and Arenas
When they keep the price of tickets down, the cost of parking goes up.

## The Stadium Service Principle

The quality of food and service varies inversely with the number of alternative sources available.

*Corollary*

When there is only one concessionaire, the price will be exorbitant.

## The McGwire Principle

The biggest plays occur when you're out buying beer.

## Emily's Rule of Sporting Events (the Super Bowl Principle)

The more highly anticipated the sporting event, the less exciting it will be.

## First Law of Spelunking

Never try to crawl through a hole smaller than your head.

## Irv's Law of Golf

Any swing improvement will only last three holes.

## Taylor's Putting Principle

Any putt is straight if you hit it hard enough.

## Gross's Law of Golf

Demo clubs only work until you buy them.

**Felt's Law of Golf**
The first time you three-putt will be on the first green you hit in regulation.

**Bloch's Law**
The only time your ball listens to you when you're yelling at it is when you're giving it misinformation.

**Sid's Law**
You can't win them all if you don't win the first one.

**O. J.'s Law**
It doesn't matter if you win or lose . . . until you lose.

# LEgAL mURPHology

### Jefferson's Prescient Principle
It is the trade of lawyers to question everything, yield nothing, and to talk by the hour.

### Oppenheimer's Precept
Ignorance of the law does not prevent a losing lawyer from collecting his bill.

### Parsons's Law
In a town where one lawyer can't survive, two lawyers will thrive.

### Dalton's Law
A bad lawyer can let a case drag on for several years. A good lawyer can make it last even longer.

## The Lawyer Joke Law
The problem with lawyer jokes is that lawyers don't think they're funny, and nobody else thinks they're jokes.

## Mr. Mendelson's Law
Ten percent of your clients give you 90 percent of your grief.

## Chisholm's Distinction
A contingent fee means that a lawyer who doesn't win your suit gets nothing. If the lawyer does win it, you get nothing.

## The Shoemaker's Children Principle
Law firms' corporate papers are never in order.

## Storry's Principle of Criminal Indictment
The degree of guilt is directly proportional to the intensity of the denial.

## Mercado's Law
After getting a client off on a grand theft auto charge, he will steal your car.

## Drew's Law of Professional Practice
The client who pays the least complains the most.

## Gualtieri's Law of Inertia
Where there's a will, there's a won't.

### The Lawyer's Maxim
Where there's a will, there's a lawsuit.

### Green's Rule
What the large print giveth, the small print taketh away.

### Rooney's Rule
Nothing in fine print is ever good news.

### Mishlove's Law
Never trust a lawyer who says he just slapped something together.

### Gibb's Law
Infinity is one lawyer waiting for another.

### Kline's Rule of Contract Law
The one document that is missing will contain the information upon which all other documents depend.

### Laws of Contract Negotiations
1. Each unacceptable offer has an equal and opposite unreasonable demand.
2. Any concession won is offset by a concession granted.

### Cunningham's Law of Contracts
The party for whom proposed changes are unacceptable will be the last party to review the document.

## Lucas's Law of Negotiation
A negotiation shall be considered successful if all parties walk away feeling screwed.

## Judge Fanin's Law
Liability follows damages.

## The Awful Truth
Estate planning is not intended to protect your estate if you die. It is intended to protect your estate *when* you die.

## Mendelson's Laws
1. No case settles before it is fully billed.
2. There is no such thing as "our" attorney.

## Andrew Young's Rule
Nothing is illegal if a hundred businessmen decide to do it.

## McCandlish's Law of Unjust Bureaucracy
Any system of justice in which ignorance of the law is no exception, but in which there are too many laws for any one person to know and remember, is by definition unjust.

## Sprecht's Rule of Law
Under any conditions, anywhere, whatever you are doing, there is some ordinance under which you can be booked.

## Solomon's Solution
Always provide your adversary two options, one of which is much worse than the one you are seeking.

## Gross's Courtroom Laws
1. If you are early for a court appearance, the judge will be late; if you are late for a court appearance, the judge will be on time.
2. Even if your case is the first case on a long court calendar, it will be the last one heard—unless you are late.

## Gross's Trial Preparation Principle
The more thoroughly you prepare for a trial, the greater the chance of a continuance.

## Murphy's Second Law for Defense Attorneys
The juror you fought hardest to retain will be the one hold-out for conviction.

## Courtney's Courthouse Codicil
The degree of attention paid by the jury is inversely proportional to the importance of the evidence.

## Henderson's Law
The less you say, the less you have to retract.

**Billing's Law**
Silence is one of the hardest things to refute.

**Bergen's Law**
There's nothing worse than a stupid law.

**Rosa's Law Office Laws**
1. Clients calling for appointments never have their appointment books in front of them.
2. The phone never rings until you've just dialed a number on the other line.

**Law of Supercession**
In court, Murphy's Law supersedes local, state, and federal law.

# MEdICAL mURPHology

### Stoeker's Lemma
If your time ain't come, not even a doctor can kill you.

### Davies's Law of Medical Relativity
If your condition seems to be getting better, it's probably your doctor getting sick.

### The Clinic Principle
The longer you spend in the waiting room, the greater the likelihood that you will be sent to another room to begin waiting again.

### Levine's Law
You always urinate just before they ask you for a urine sample.

## Lyall's Principle for Patients
Just because your doctors have a name for your condition doesn't mean they know what it is.

## Warner's Prescription Principles
1. Only adults have difficulty with childproof bottles.
2. You never have the right number of pills left on the last day of a prescription.
3. The pills to be taken with meals will be the least appetizing ones.

## Matz's Warning
Beware of the physician who is great at getting out of trouble.

## Barach's Rule
An alcoholic is a person who drinks more than his own physician.

## Hodgins's Homily
A miracle drug is any drug that will do what the label says it will do.

## Schick's Lament
It is too bad that we cannot cut the patient in half in order to compare two regimens of treatment.

## Howland's Law for Physicians

You never catch your patient's cold until you're about to leave on vacation.

## Barron's Law

When a doctor gets ill it will be in the area of his own specialty.

## Dolman's First Law

The first time you screw up a colonoscopy, your patient is a lawyer.

## Cochrane's Aphorism

Before ordering a test, decide what you will do if it is (1) positive, or (2) negative. If both answers are the same, don't do the test.

## Bernstein's Precept

The radiologists' national flower is the hedge.

## Meltzer's Law of Diagnosis

The fact that your patient gets well does not prove that your diagnosis was correct.

## Law of Health Fads

No matter how often a health fad has been shown to be ineffective, there will remain a percentage of people who believe in it.

### Corollary

The more absurd the fad, the more resolute the believers.

## First Rule for Nurses
Never let the doctors know you know more than they do.

## Sullivan's Nursing Law
Unexpected breaks in your workload always coincide with unexpected patient emergencies.

## Sweeney's Law
Emergencies only occur on days when you have left your pager at home.

## Margot's Nursing Maxims
1. You always find yourself working with the doctor you like the least.
2. If you make a mistake in front of a doctor, you are sure to encounter that doctor at least three more times during your shift.
3. The colleague you don't get along with will be made supervisor.

## Telesco's Laws of Nursing
1. All the IVs are at the other end of the hall.
2. A physician's ability is inversely proportional to his availability.
3. There are two kinds of adhesive tape: that which won't stay on and that which won't come off.
4. Everybody wants a pain shot at the same time.

5. Everybody who didn't want a pain shot when you were passing out pain shots wants one when you are passing out sleeping pills.

## First Rule for Interns
Never say "I'm new at this" to a patient.

## Bulf's Law
The more urgent the transfusion, the rarer the blood type.

## The Night Nurse Rule
The nurse from hell only shows up in your room when your family and friends are gone.

## Hospital Room Rules
1. The bedpan is always just out of reach.

### Corollary
If you manage to reach it, it spills.

2. The only time you can find the call button is when you press it accidentally.
3. The more urgently you need to go the bathroom, the more tangled your IV line.
4. As soon as you get to sleep, someone will wake you up to give you a sleeping pill.
5. Every hospital employee assumes that every patient is hard-of-hearing.
6. The better your appetite, the worse the food.

# cONSUMERology

**Law of Regressive Achievement**

Last year's was always better.

**Herblock's Law**

If it's good, they discontinue it.

**Gold's Law**

If the shoe fits, it's ugly.

**Hadley's Laws of Clothing Shopping**

1. If you like it, they don't have it in your size.
2. If you like it and it's in your size, it doesn't fit anyway.
3. If you like it and it fits, you can't afford it.
4. If you like it, it fits, and you can afford it, it falls apart the first time you wear it.

## Finman's Bargain Basement Principle
The one you want is never the one on sale.

## Lewis's Law
No matter how long or how hard you shop for an item, after you've bought it, it will be on sale somewhere cheaper.

## Hershiser's Rules
1. Anything labeled "NEW" and/or "IMPROVED" isn't.
2. The label "NEW" and/or "IMPROVED" means the price went up.
3. The label "ALL NEW," "COMPLETELY NEW," or "GREAT NEW" means the price went way up.

## McGowan's Madison Avenue Axiom
If an item is advertised as "under $50," you can bet it's not $19.95.

## Murray's Laws
1. Never ask a barber if you need a haircut.
2. Never ask a salesman if his is a good price.

## Glaser's Law
If it says "one size fits all," it doesn't fit anyone.

## Sintetos's Law of Consumerism
A sixty-day warranty guarantees that the product will self-destruct on the sixty-first day.

**Beryl's Law**

The *Consumer Reports* article on the item will come out a week after you've made your purchase.

*Corollaries*

1. The one you bought will be rated "unacceptable."
2. The one you almost bought will be rated "best buy."

**Savignano's Mail-Order Law**

If you don't write to complain, you'll never receive your order.

If you do write, you'll receive the merchandise before your angry letter reaches its destination.

**Yount's Back-Order Principle**

During the time an item is back-ordered, it will be available more cheaply and quickly from many other sources.

**Lewis's Law**

People will buy anything that's one to a customer.

**Brooks's Law of Retailing**

Security isn't.

Management can't.

Sales promotions don't.

Consumer assistance doesn't.

Workers won't.

**Gerhardt's Law**

If you find something you like, buy a lifetime supply. They are going to stop making it.

**Helen's Law of Bargain Shopping**

If you don't buy it when you first see it, it won't be there when you come back.

**Murphy's Law of Supply**

If you don't need it and don't want it, there is always plenty of it.

**Czliknsky's Law of Retail**

If you want to browse, you will be inundated by clerks; if you want to buy, no clerk can be found.

**Booth's Grocery Store Principle**

Regardless of the product you are looking for, someone else's shopping cart will be in front of it.

**Walker's Law**

Urgency varies inversely with value.

**Paulsen's Rule**

Enter a contest and be on the sponsor's sucker list for life.

## The Gluskin-Fagan Rules
1. Takeovers are always announced one day after you sell the stock of the target company.
2. Time-tested investment strategies stop working as soon as you put your money into them.
3. The next bull market will begin on the day you swear never to touch another stock as long as you live.
4. The only hot stock-market tips that work are those you have ignored.

## Robbin's Rules of Marketing
1. Your share of the market is lower than you think.
2. The combined market position goals of all competitors always totals at least 150 percent.
3. The existence of a market does not ensure the existence of a customer.
4. Beware of alleged needs that have no real market.
5. Low price and long shipment will win over high price and short shipment.
6. If the customer buys lunch, you've lost the order.

## Murray's Law
Don't believe everything you hear or anything you say.

## Fredericks's Laws of Marketing
1. Never listen to your own hype.
2. Never get downwind from your marketing.

**Third Rule for Retailers**
The customer is almost right.

**The Law of Oversell**
When putting cheese in a mousetrap, always leave room for the mouse.

**Say's Law**
Supply creates its own demand.

**Panger's Advertising Principle**
Nobody buys a half-truth, but some will swallow a whole lie.

**First Rule of Foreign Sales**
Any foreign payments will be at the worst possible exchange rate.

**The Banking Principle**
When you get to the front of the line, the teller will close.
*Corollary*
The "Use Next Window" sign will point to a window that is also closed.

# mURPHology aND THe ArTS

**Ely's Law**
Wear the right costume and the part plays itself.

**First Rule of Acting**
Whatever happens, look as if it was intended.

**Jones's Law of Publishing**
Some errors will always go unnoticed until the book is in print.
*Bloch's Corollary*
The first page the author turns to upon receiving an advance copy will be the page containing the worst error.

## Photographer's Laws

1. The best shots happen immediately after the last frame is exposed.
2. The other best shots are generally attempted through the lens cap.

## Dowling's Law of Photography

One missed photographic opportunity creates a desire to purchase two additional pieces of equipment.

## Deitz's Law of Ego

The fury engendered by the misspelling of a name in a column is in direct ratio to the obscurity of the mentionee.

## Fuller's Law of Journalism

The farther away the disaster or accident occurs, the greater the number of dead and injured required for it to become a story.

## Gold's Law of Journalism

A column about errors will contain errors.

## Jones's Law

Originality is the art of concealing your source.

## Wallace Wood's Rule of Drawing

1. Never draw what you can copy.
2. Never copy what you can trace.
3. Never trace what you can cut out and paste down.

## Twain on Facts
Get your facts first, and then you can distort them as much as you please.

## T. S. Eliot's Observation
Some editors are failed writers, but so are most writers.

## The Decorative Artwork Principle
The cost for the framing exceeds the cost of the art.
### Sussman's Corollary
People who bargain over the price of the art will not bargain over the price charged by the framer.

## Schmidt's Guide to Art
Sculpture is what you bump into when you back up to look at a painting.

## Laws for Freelance Artists
1. A high-paying rush job comes in only after you have committed to a low-paying rush job.
2. All rush jobs are due the same day.
3. The rush job you spent all night on won't be needed for at least two days.

## Carson's Laws of Comedy
1. If they buy the premise, they'll buy the bit.
2. Don't do more than three jokes on the same premise.

## Law of Talent Shows

The best performer in your category will go on just before you do.

## Yellin's Theater Law

The tallest person in the audience will sit down in front of you only after it is too late for you to find another seat.

## Chekhov's Law

If there is a gun hanging on the wall in the first act, it must fire in the last.

## Butner's Law

He who laughs last thinks slowest.

# mURPHology OF TImE

**Finnigan's Law**
The farther away the future is, the better it looks.

**Simon's Law of Destiny**
Glory may be fleeting, but obscurity is forever.

**Bombeck's Law of Heredity**
Insanity is hereditary; you get it from your kids.

**Kelly's Observation**
Living in the past has one thing in its favor—it's cheaper.

**Capp's Law**
The closest you can get to your youth is to start repeating your follies.

**Dumper's Principle of Neoteny**
An adult is a deteriorated child.

**Anderson's Axiom**
You can only be young once, but you can be immature forever.

**Carillo's Codicil**
Age is a high price to pay for maturity.

**Maury's Law**
No one is too old to learn a new way of being stupid.

**Elliott's Axiom**
All children are future ex-idealists.

**The Interest Principle**
Almost everything is more popular than it used to be.

**Pierson's Law**
If you're coasting, you're going downhill.

**Nitzberg's Law**
A home is ruled by the sickest person in it.

**Tallulah Bankhead's Observation**
If I had to live my life again, I'd make the same mistakes, only sooner.

### Ertz's Observation
Millions long for immortality who don't know what to do on a rainy Sunday afternoon.

### Grimes's Law
Nostalgia is the realization that things weren't as unbearable as they seemed at the time.

### Kubin's Maxim
How feeble are Man's efforts against the unyielding forces of Nature—until the struggle is recounted for the grandchildren.

### Twain's Observation
If you abstain from drinking, smoking, and carousing, you may not live longer—but it will feel longer.

### Russell's Rule
Don't worry about avoiding temptation—as you grow older, it starts avoiding you.

### Shaw's Maxim
Virtue is insufficient temptation.

### Peterson's Principle
Traditions are solutions for which we have forgotten the problems.

### Baker's Bylaw
When you are over the hill, you pick up speed.

**Linus's Law**

There is no heavier burden than a great potential.

**Huxley on Progress**

Technological progress has merely provided us with more efficient means for going backwards.

**Ogden Nash's Law**

Progress may have been all right once, but it went on too long.

**Ellis's Law**

Progress is the exchange of one nuisance for another.

**Engler's Rule of Innovation**

Innovation requires bypassing—not building upon—existing expertise.

**Law of Survival**

It's not who is right, it's who is left.

**Gerhard's Observation**

We're making progress. Things are getting worse at a slower rate.

**Jerry's Law**

Just because everything is different doesn't mean anything has changed.

# PsYCHO-mURPHology

## O'Brien's Law
Nothing is ever done for the right reasons.

## Glyme's Formula for Success
The secret of success is sincerity. Once you can fake that, you've got it made.

## Helga's Rule
Say no, then negotiate.

## Professor Block's Motto
Forgive and remember.

## Jacob's Law
To err is human—to blame it on someone else is even more human.

**Edelstein's Advice**
Don't worry over what other people are thinking about you. They're too busy worrying over what you are thinking about them.

**The Fifth Rule**
You have taken yourself too seriously.

**Sartre's Observation**
Hell is others.

**Pascal on Man**
The more I see of men, the better I like my dog.

**Salk's Law**
The secret to happiness is to rely on as few other people as possible.

**Cromer's Law**
People who don't believe in anything will believe the worst of other people.

**La Rochefoucauld's Rule**
We all have the strength to endure the misfortune of others.

**Howe's Theory**
There is some advice that is too good—the advice to love your enemies, for example.

**Morris's Law**
Anyone can admit to themselves they were wrong—the true test is admitting it to someone else.

**Jerome's Rule**
It is always the best policy to speak the truth—unless of course you are an exceptionally good liar.

**Tomlin's Truism**
Man invented language to satisfy his deep need to complain.

**Mizner's Law**
Misery loves company, but company does not reciprocate.

**Maugham's Observation**
It is easier to give up good habits than bad ones.

**Arlen's Law**
It's amazing how nice people are to you when they know you're going away.

**Zappa's Law**
There are two things on earth that are universal: hydrogen and stupidity.

**First Principle of Self-Determination**
What you resist, you become.

**Milliken's Maxim**
Insanity is doing the same thing the same way and expecting different results.

**Gutierrez's Law**
True freedom is freedom from choice.

**The Bering Distinction**
Philosophy is questions that may never be answered.
Religion is answers that may never be questioned.

**Dick's Lemma**
Just because you're paranoid doesn't mean they're not out to get you.

**Larson's Law**
A lot of people mistake a short memory for a clear conscience.

**Santayana's First Law**
Sanity is madness put to good use.

**W. C. Field's Maxim**
Start every day off with a smile and get it over with.

# ThEOREtICAL mURPHology

**Murphy's Law of Research**

Enough research will tend to support your theory.

**Maier's Law**

If the facts do not conform to the theory, they must be disposed of.

***Corollaries***

1. The bigger the theory, the better.
2. The experiment may be considered a success if no more than 50 percent of the observed measurements must be discarded to obtain a correspondence with the theory.

**Clarke's Law of Revolutionary Ideas**

Every revolutionary area—in science, politics, art, or whatever—evokes three stages of reaction. They may be summed up by the three phrases:

1. "It is impossible—don't waste my time."
2. "It is possible, but it is not worth doing."
3. "I said it was a good idea all along."

## Rule of the Great

When somebody you greatly admire and respect appears to be thinking deep thoughts, he is probably thinking about lunch.

## Clarke's Third Law

Any sufficiently advanced technology is indistinguishable from magic.

## Storman's Law

An idea is not responsible for the people who believe in it.

## Law of Superiority

The first example of superior principle is always inferior to the developed example of inferior principle.

## Baker's Rule

Inanimate objects are classified scientifically into three major categories: those that don't work, those that break down, and those that get lost.

## Blaauw's Law

Established technology tends to persist in spite of new technology.

**Everitt's Law of Thermodynamics**
Confusion is always increasing in society. Only if someone or something works extremely hard can this confusion be reduced to order in a limited region. Nevertheless, this effort will still result in an increase in the total confusion of society at large.

**Levy's Second Law**
Only God can make a random selection.

**Meyer's Law**
It is a simple task to make things complex, but a complex task to make them simple.

**Hlade's Law**
If you have a difficult task, give it to a lazy man—he will find an easier way to do it.

**Hunt's Law**
Every great idea has a disadvantage equal to or exceeding the greatness of the idea.

**Macbeth's Comment on Evolution**
The best theory is not ipso facto a good theory.

**Barr's Inertial Principle**
Asking a group of scientists to revise their theory is like asking a group of cops to revise the law.

## The Sagan Fallacy

To say a human being is nothing but molecules is like saying a Shakespearean play is nothing but words.

## The Reliability Principle

The difference between the Laws of Nature and Murphy's Law is that with the Laws of Nature you can count on things screwing up the same way every time.

## Darwin's Law

Nature will tell you a direct lie if she can.

### Bloch's Extension

So will Darwinists.

## First Law of Scientific Progress

The advance of science can be measured by the rate at which exceptions to previously held laws accumulate.

### Corollaries

1. Exceptions always outnumber rules.
2. There are always exceptions to established exceptions.
3. By the time one masters the exceptions, no one recalls the rules to which they apply.

## Jones's Law

Anyone who makes a significant contribution to any field of endeavor, and stays in that field long enough, becomes an obstruction to its progress—in direct proportion to the importance of his original contribution.

## Mann's Law (Generalized)
If a scientist uncovers a publishable fact, it will become central to his theory.
### Corollary
This theory, in turn, will become central to all scientific thought.

## Grelb's Law of Erroring
In any series of calculations, errors tend to occur at the opposite end from which you begin checking.

## Robert's Axiom
Only errors exist.
### Berman's Corollary
One man's error is another man's data.

## Last Law of Robotics
The only real errors are human errors.

## Young's Law
It is when you trip over your own shoes that you start picking up shoes.

## Hoffer's Law
When people are free to do as they please, they usually imitate each other.

## Perlsweig's Law
Whatever goes around, comes around.

### *Les Misérables* Metalaw
All laws, whether good, bad, or indifferent, must be obeyed to the letter.

### Persig's Postulate
The number of rational hypotheses that can explain any given phenomenon is infinite.

### Lilly's Metalaw
All laws are simulations of reality.

### The Ultimate Principle
By definition, when you are investigating the unknown, you do not know what you will find.

### Cooper's Metalaw
A proliferation of new laws creates a proliferation of new loopholes.

### Digiovanni's Law
The number of laws will expand to fill the publishing space available.

### Jaffe's Precept
There are some things that are impossible to know—but it is impossible to know these things.

**Muir's Law**
When we try to pick out anything by itself, we find it hitched to everything else in the universe.

**Cole's Law**
Thinly sliced cabbage.

**Welwood's Axiom**
Disorder expands proportionately to the tolerance for it.

**The Aquinas Axiom**
What the gods get away with, the cows don't.

**White's Chappaquiddick Theorem**
The sooner and in more detail you announce the bad news, the better.

**The Last Law**
It's better to have a horrible ending than to have horrors without end.

**Matsch's Law**
If several things that could have gone wrong have not gone wrong, it would have been ultimately beneficial for them to have gone wrong.

**Finagle's Law According to Niven**
The perversity of the universe tends to a maximum.

## Long's Law
Natural laws have no pity.

## Ulmann's Razor
When stupidity is a sufficient explanation, there is no need to have recourse to any other.

## Dyer's Law of Relativity
Life is short, but a three-hour movie is interminable.

# tRANSCenDENtAL mURPHology

**James's Principle**
There is no greater lie than a truth misunderstood.

**Horace's Warning**
Beware of the superficially profound.

**Puddinhead's Lemma**
Faith is believin' what you know ain't so.

**Holmes's Homily**
It is well to remember that the entire universe, with one trifling exception, is composed of others.

**Wilde on Man and God**
God, in creating man, somewhat overestimated his ability.

**Heisenberg's Law**
There are things that are so serious that you can only joke about them.

**Russell's Observation**
The point of philosophy is to start with something so simple as to seem not worth stating, and to end with something so paradoxical that no one will believe it.

**Toynbee's Rule**
In matters of religion, it is very easy to deceive mankind and very difficult to undeceive them.

**Father Fitzgerald's Rule**
Behave as if you were watched.

**Sauget's Law**
Sit at the feet of the master long enough and they start to smell.

**Millay's Maxim**
It is not true that life is one damn thing after another—it's one damn thing over and over.

**Defalque's Observation**
A path without obstacles usually leads nowhere.

**Mumford's Maxim**
Traditionalists are pessimists about the future and optimists about the past.

**Rostand's Comment**
My pessimism extends to the point of even suspecting the sincerity of other pessimists.

**Aquinas's Warning**
Beware the man of one book.

**The Old Porter's Observation**
There's very few what comes up to the average.

**Berra's Advice**
When you come to a fork in the road, take it.

**Friedman's Observation**
Human beings are distinguished from other animals more by their ability to rationalize than by their ability to reason.

**The Voice-Mail Principle**
Those whom the gods wish to destroy, they first put on hold.

**Tomlin's Law**
Reality is nothing but a collective hunch.

## P. K. Dick's Rule
Reality is what refuses to go away when you stop believing in it.

## R. A. Wilson's Rule
Reality is whatever you can get away with.

## Einstein on Life
1. Reality is merely an illusion, albeit a very persistent one.
2. Imagination is more important than knowledge.
3. The only real valuable thing is intuition.
4. Everything should be made as simple as possible, but not simpler.
5. Common sense is the collection of prejudices acquired by age eighteen.
6. Gravitation is not responsible for people falling in love.

## Kegley's Law
If a pickpocket meets a saint, he sees only his pockets.

## Wilde's Theory
Only the shallow know themselves.

## Roosevelt's Rule
When you get to the end of your rope, tie a knot and hang on.

### Clarke's Law of Evolution
It has yet to be proven that intelligence has any survival value.

### Syrus's Axiom
Not every question deserves an answer.

### Voltaire's Maxim
A witty saying proves nothing.

Arthur Bloch is the author of 10 *Murphy's Law* books, which have been published in more than 30 countries and have sold millions of copies worldwide. He also wrote a self-help satire, *Healing Yourself with Wishful Thinking*. Since 1986 he has been producer/director of the *Thinking Allowed* public television series. Bloch runs Hypersphere, an Internet design company. He lives in Oakland, California with his wife, Barbara.